Around the world under water
CAPTAIN EDWARD L. BEACH

Britannica Bookshelf—Great Lives for Young Americans

Around the world under water

CAPTAIN EDWARD L. BEACH

by *Beril Becker*

Illustrated by Richard Mlodock

Published by
ENCYCLOPAEDIA BRITANNICA PRESS, Chicago

TABLE OF CONTENTS

Around the world under water
CAPTAIN EDWARD L. BEACH

ROUTE OF THE *TRITON*

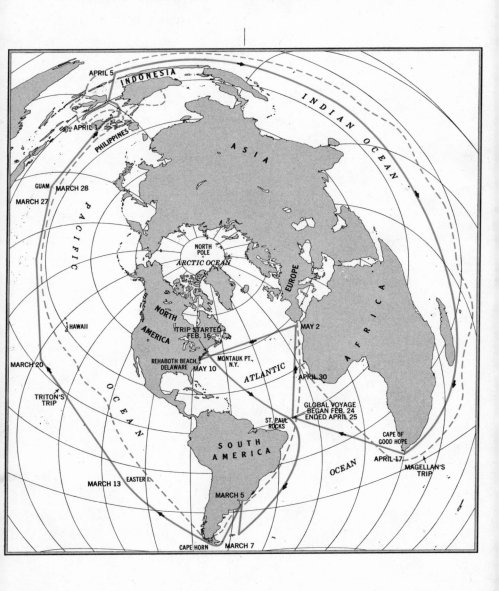

Chapter *1*

Project Magellan

A submarine as long as two city blocks and as high as a four-story building was launched into the Thames River at Groton, Connecticut on August 18, 1958.

As the huge, cigar-shaped hull poised on the launching dock, painted a strange combination of vivid orange and green, it had all the weird appearance of a science-fiction spaceship from another planet. It seemed incredible that this futuristic 1990 model had actually become a reality in 1958.

The greatest crowd ever assembled at a submarine launching, about 35,000, sensed the historical importance of the occasion. Scarcely two weeks earlier, on August 3, the first atomic submarine, the *Nautilus*, had crossed the North Pole under the Arctic ice. The nuclear *Skate* had cracked through the ice of the North Pole itself on August 11. These events were dramatic proofs that a new age of technology had arrived. Now the latest wonder of the nuclear submarines, the *Triton*, loomed up with impressive proportions to re-emphasize America's might.

The Prospective Commanding Officer stood at attention on the bridge above the men in Navy white lined up on deck. It was a proud day for the man who had been chosen to command the giant of all submarines. He had been picked out of an eligible group of 138 skippers of submarines who had combat experience in World War II.

The largest submarine in the world seemed destined to come under the command of this officer. The great tradition of the U. S. Navy was bred in his bones. His father had served under Admiral Dewey and had been advanced to the command of the battleship *New York*. The father had written many stories of Navy life for children, and it could be said that his son, Ned, had begun his naval life when he began to read.

It was inevitable that the son should follow his father's footsteps through the Naval Academy at Annapolis. Ned Beach graduated in 1939, just in time to help defend his country in a dozen war patrols against the Japanese. Very few submariners endured as much battle experience and survived to tell about it. At the age of 27, he was the skipper of his own submarine, and the publication of his book *Submarine* after the war brought him nationwide literary prominence. His next book, the novel *Run Silent, Run Deep*, also became a national best seller and was made into a movie starring Clark Gable and Burt Lancaster. Captain Beach went on to become Naval Aide to General Omar Bradley and later to President Eisenhower.

The launching ceremony ended when an Admiral's wife smashed a bottle of champagne against the hull and christened the ship *USS Triton*. The massive bulk, under a rainbow of flags and pennants from bow to stern, slipped into the Thames River. Tugs pushed her to the fitting-out docks of the Electric Boat Company just across the river from New London, Connecticut.

Decked with flags, the Triton was launched into the Thames.

Now the *Triton* was to go through its second stage. It was to be supplied with an atomic heart, with electronic eyes and ears, and with the keenest system of nerves ever wired into a submarine.

At that time, there was a mood of crisis and urgency in the great submarine yards. The U. S. Navy had pulled all stops to forge ahead with the new Polaris submarine system of defense. Neither the solid propellant to shoot a Polaris rocket out of water nor the missile itself with its automatic guiding system had yet been perfected. But the Navy decided to follow Admiral Hyman Rickover's method of putting faith in the competence of good engineers. These

[13]

men had become the miracle men of the age and were expected to find the answer to every problem.

To build the first Polaris submarine the Navy ordered a partially built atomic submarine to be sliced in half, and the bow moved forward 130 feet. A missile section was inserted in the middle and the three pieces of submarine were welded together. Three shifts worked around the clock seven days a week to complete that first Polaris submarine— the *George Washington*. Because of the top priority of the Polaris project, the *Triton* was not to be equipped and ready for sea until many months later than originally planned.

The readying period for the *Triton* progressed at a snail's pace, or so it seemed to the Captain and crew. The commissioning ceremony came late in 1959. The title of Captain Beach changed from "Prospective Commanding Officer" or "Officer-in-Charge" to simply "Commanding Officer." The sea trials were successful and the ship was ready at last for the final stage—the shakedown cruise.

Then another plague of delays descended upon the *Triton*. Instead of shakedown orders, the Captain's mail contained all kinds of promotion and transfer orders. Men perfectly trained for *Triton* duty were ordered to leave. New officers arrived. The Polaris program seemed to be playing havoc with the Captain's plans for a perfectly trained crew.

What was even more mystifying was the new equipment that kept arriving which required more installation work and additional men to operate it. There were more sea trials, but when the *Triton* returned to New London on February 1, 1960, a letter was waiting which Captain Beach was certain was the ship's shakedown orders. When he tore open the envelope, inside was a note from Rear Admiral L. R. Daspit, the Atlantic Fleet Submarine Force Commander, asking Beach to come to Washington on February 4. The mystery deepened when he was asked to come in "civvies." "What now?" the Captain chafed.

The conference was held in the office of the Deputy Chief of Naval Operations for Fleet Operations. The long name was necessary to identify a particular department in the world's largest office building—the Pentagon. Captain Beach, wearing civilian clothes, knew that something important was up when he faced a battery of top Navy officers, also mysteriously dressed in "civvies."

Vice Admiral Wallace M. Beakley came directly to the point.

"Beach, you're about to start your shakedown cruise. Can *Triton* go around the world—submerged—instead?"

Stunned by this extraordinary demand, Captain Beach could only gasp, "Yes, sir!" Beach was known to keep a tight control over himself as well as his ships, and no one suspected the leaping excitement within him.

"When can you get under way?"

After many months of all kinds of delays, the Captain was asked to start a brand-new submarine on a maiden voyage around the world as soon as possible. Beach recalled his plebe days at Annapolis, when the first-year men were not allowed to say, "I don't know, sir." Navy discipline demanded that they say, "I'll find out, sir!"

There was a long pause as Beach thought over the

[15]

situation. Loading adequate food supplies alone might take days. The study of hydrographic charts could consume an equal number of days. There would be a mountain of paper work to prepare. He would have to work the crew around the clock to get everything done. He said he would be ready to sail in 12 days.

The long discussions that followed made several things clear to the Captain. Plans for the *Triton* had been held up to see if the Polaris program could make its technical breakthroughs. And to everybody's great relief, the engineers had come through.

Solid propellants for missiles could now function efficiently. Compressed air could pop out a missile from a Polaris submarine like a cork from a champagne bottle. It blasted up through the water and a hundred feet into the air. A timing device touched off the first-stage rocket. The guidance system set the rocket on a true course. After the solid propellant burned out, the cone was separated 120 miles up, and zoomed ahead to its pinpointed destination at 12,000 miles an hour. Polaris submarines would be plowing the depths sooner than expected. A new underwater frontier had opened up for the Navy.

This was the reason for the sudden decision to send the *Triton* around the world. There was a need for all kinds of new information about sea currents, about how long a nuclear sub could stay under water, about the ability of man to endure long confinement in an artificial atmosphere.

The *Triton* was to investigate these mysteries and others. For example, a half-pound dynamite explosion in the sea had been detected 3,000 miles away. Another explosion set off in Australia was heard in Bermuda, 12,000 miles away. Was there a natural "speaking tube" that could be used around the world?

A new world of sonar communication might be developed. Just as a radio or radar operator can detect air traffic, could not a sonar operator be able to listen in on a worldwide system that would reveal the course, speed, and location of any submarine anywhere in the world? Could not a sonarman develop a sixth sense to identify any individual object under water? Would it be possible to develop a dictionary of "noise signatures" that would identify any individual ship by the pitch and sound of its propellers?

If all the undersea streams of the seven oceans could be charted in detail, the captain of a submarine would know where and when he could shut off his power and float along these flowing rivers underneath the surface. A sub skipper under enemy attack by a surface vessel could check a future hydrographic manual and find the depth which would permit him to drift away on a thermocline, the line that separates cold and warm layers of water.

After hearing what the Navy would like to discover Captain Beach was then given a survey of all possible dangers. Undersea charts were far from complete. There was a real risk of running into uncharted undersea mountains, just as ancient mariners ran into uncharted rocks. There was the possibility the *Triton* might meet with avalanches of silt-laden water caused by earthquakes. A chain of underwater volcanoes circling the Southern Pacific Ocean could erupt at any moment. Despite these dangers, the *Triton*

[17]

was to gather all kinds of information about the depths of the sea.

Most important, perhaps, would be the testing of morale among crew members. The *Triton* voyage could determine their breaking point, and this in turn would determine the future planning of the Polaris program. The voyage would determine whether Polaris subs could travel halfway around the world to fire their missiles and return without surfacing. It might be found wiser to use submarine tenders specially equipped to bring duplicate crews and provisions to a Polaris fleet in order to keep them at sea continuously within their battle areas. The *Triton* would determine how often the renewal of men and supplies to Polaris subs would have to arrive.

Many other questions were posed. Seven scientists would be sent aboard to make necessary investigations in their respective fields.

The circumnavigation would follow a route that almost paralleled that of Magellan, whose ships were the first to circle the globe. Hence, the round-the-world voyage would be officially called Project Magellan. The *Triton* would have to follow a strict time schedule. Since it would not be allowed to surface, Navy headquarters in Washington would have to know its whereabouts from day to day. A rescue party would then know what area to search in case of an emergency or accident.

The Magellan touch appealed to the Captain, who was a man of imagination. He suggested that the *Triton* should reach the point in the Philippines where Magellan was killed and also pass close to Cadiz, Spain, where Magellan

[18]

started. The historic value of the *Triton* voyage would be enhanced if a memorial of some sort, perhaps a plaque, were designed and given to the government of Spain. These suggestions from Beach were accepted. The circumnavigation was rerouted to include Magellan's starting and finishing points.

Captain Beach returned to New London both exalted and concerned. He felt a pang in not being able to tell his family anything about his top secret mission. Most of the crew had wives and children. How was he to keep the secret from 175 crew members? They would have to be told that the *Triton* had been ordered to ninety-day maneuvers without returning to base. Arrangements would have to be made to send their pay checks to their families and to postpone automobile licenses and income-tax returns. There would be a deluge of paper work.

When the officers were gathered at a secret meeting and told the truth about the mission, there were whistles of incredulity. Who ever heard of a voyage around the world for a shakedown cruise? But they were highly excited. It is not every year that one has an opportunity to play a role in history.

Later that same day, the Captain spoke to the assembled crew over the loudspeaker system. He broke the news that they might have to be away for ninety days or more. They would have to fill out sheets of "Things to Do." They were to sign the sheets and return them only after completing the paper work specified in the instructions.

The crew accepted the assignment without murmuring. Submariners are a special, hearty breed of men.

No one ever tried to explain how the many truck-loads of provisions that kept arriving day after day were ever stowed away. The submarine already appeared to be jammed full. But like the dozen college students stuffed into a telephone booth, the feat was somehow accomplished. Crates of special equipment looked suspicious, but no one asked embarrassing questions. The Diving Officer, Tom B. Thamm, also an artist, designed the Magellan plaque, which was sent away to be cast in shiny brass.

In addition to briefing 175 men, listening to problems of officers who lined up for interviews, scrutinizing hundreds of reports, signing his name to an avalanche of papers, the skipper had to study foot-high piles of charts that covered the surface of the globe. The Navigator outlined the route in precise latitude and longitude points, timing each day's distance to the exact minute.

The considerable amount of personal luggage that arrived on the morning of departure started a chain of speculation, heightened by the arrival of the seven scientists soon after. But when the gangplank was raised in the early afternoon of the 16th of February, 1960, the skipper was sure that only he and certain trusted officers knew of the secret mission. Final preparations had been completed in the record time of 12 days.

As the *Triton* sped down the Thames, the Captain kept one eye fixed on a distant rock on top of a hill. There he saw the tiny figure of his wife, etched against the sky, waving her handkerchief, and his throat filled up. He was glad she did not know the formidable challenge of the

The Captain stood in the conning tower as the Triton sped to sea.

shakedown voyage. He waved back until she could no longer be seen.

The *Triton* cut its way over the Atlantic, its two huge propellers driving at full speed over the 150 miles of the continental shelf, across the forty-mile stretch of the Gulf Stream, far away from the much traveled shipping lanes.

By sunset, he climbed down the conning tower into the control room. The graphic pen of the fathometer indicated that the ocean floor was deep enough for submergence. He lifted a phone and snapped out his command, "Take her down!"

Two alarms blasted out instantly. The men on watch raced down from the bridge in scheduled order, the last man closing the hatch after him. "Hatch secure!" The cry was confirmed on the control panel where two bars automatically aligned themselves, indicating that the last open hole in the submarine's hull was closed. At the same second, the Chief of the Watch flicked a sequence of switches on the panel before him. Vents opened in ballast tanks, and ocean water poured into space previously filled with air. As the main-ballast tanks forward filled with water, their added weight pulled the ship down into the ocean.

The planesmen operated their controls at the same time, tilting the foreplanes downward like fins, forcing the ship to bite into the water. Through the periscope the Captain saw the surface gliding steadily towards him. A quick glance at the depth gauges indicated 35 feet of submergence; only 30 seconds had passed since the blasts for clearing the bridge.

The Diving Officer spoke or motioned his signals with the sure strokes of a conductor's baton, causing men to shift levers, turn knobs, and snap switches. Within two minutes after the alarm sounded, the submarine reached its designated depth of 150 feet and leveled off for a fast tunneling run.

As soon as the *Triton* had dipped beneath the surface, Captain Beach experienced all the sensations of entering

[22]

an element that is 800 times heavier than air. The sun, the sea breezes, the hills of the earth, the colors of atmospheric life were wiped out, replaced by the fluorescent glow of the red lights in the control room.

The hurly burly of the water against the conning tower, as the ship went down, disappeared as did the noise of venting air from the ship's tanks. The spinning of the hatch handle, the turning of wheels, the swish of exhaust fans vanished into the low monotonous hum of numerous motors.

The sounds of blowers, fans, and generators combined to make a heavy background droning that became after a few moments as soundless as the ticking of a clock. Ears became adjusted to the anguished pings of the fathometer and the faint thuds of echoes bouncing back from the ocean floor. From the engine room came the distant whine of turbines and the low throbbing hum of the giant centrifugal pump.

All these muffled sounds, easily recognizable if one listened for them, were a blessed assurance to the Captain. They were the pulses of instruments that made liveable the artificial atmosphere within the capsule under the sea. As long as the instruments functioned, the Captain was assured that he would find his way back home to earth again even after going around the world.

As the *Triton* leveled off deep under the sea, tunneling ahead without slacking speed, the slight rolling and turbulence of the surface disappeared. There was no sensation. The *Triton*, like a giant sea beast, had found its true home within the undersea element. The subdued murmur of innumerable fans, the faintest rush of water flowing

[23]

past the hull, were indications to the skipper that the ship was purring ever so softly in contented ease. He pulled the curtain of his tiny cabin, turned on the electric light, and sat down to write the first entry in the log of the voyage.

Chapter *2*

Education of a Naval Captain

To Captain Beach, a ship was more than a machine. Every ship he had ever served in had a soul of its own. Often, during his war patrols, men and submarine had to endure the ordeal of depth charges. The ship itself would seem to tremble with the ague. The very air became sickly, filled with bits of cork and paint shaken out by the underwater blasts. Between the feverish seizures of hammer blows, there were intervals of silence. Men walked on tiptoe so as to make no telltale sound. Even the sub seemed to understand the need for silence. There was an almost human response as the sub barely moved its propellers, throbbing very softly, responding to orders by moving away on cat's feet. When life or death was a matter of seconds and extreme caution, the Captain knew by the response of the ship that it had a soul.

But was there a soul to the *Triton?* There were so many automatic devices and mechanical brains in the nuclear giant that Captain Beach had the feeling he might be only a cog in a mechanical monster. Would the thinking machines take over control of the ship, doing an automatic job better than he could do himself? His very crew

[25]

differed from the men he knew in previous commands. The old type of seaman had disappeared. Each member of its present crew was a highly trained technician in sonar or electronics or atomic reactors or was educating himself to be one. There was no longer a sharp difference between officers and men. Could Captain, ship, and crew ever become a single unit?

The Captain, after all, should be the indispensible heart, soul, and brain of a ship. His was the awesome responsibility of command. He, alone, would have to face the challenge of decision at the supreme moment of crisis. His split-second decision could mean life or death for the ship and crew. It might even mean victory or defeat for a nation.

It was up to the Captain to unite the 175 different personalities on board, to gain their respect, and to link them with the flying atoms of the nuclear reactor, the germanium transistors, and the zirconium coils of the ship. Only an alert unity could challenge a moment of supreme urgency.

Fortunately, the U. S. Navy had educated him for just that responsibility. It had educated his father, who was also a naval officer. The education of father and son actually parallels the story of the rise of the U. S. Navy.

As a young boy, Ned Beach grew up in Palo Alto, California, where his father was commandant of the Mare Island Naval Base. As a lad, Ned built toy submarines out of blocks of wood, weighing them down with lead to make them stay under water in the bathtub.

His interest in submarines stemmed from his father,

[26]

who had served under Admiral Dewey in the Philippine campaign of the Spanish-American War. It was Dewey who first sensed the future power of the submarine. He said that he would have been unable to defeat the enemy at Manila Bay if the Spaniards had used two submarines.

The ironclad Navy had begun only a few years before, in 1893, with three coast-defense battleships. Just about the same time it got its first submarine, John P. Holland's *Plunger*, which boasted one torpedo tube.

The submarine was a novelty during those early days. It was a valuable prop in the naval stories that the older Beach wrote for boys. In one book, published in 1911, he described how his fictional hero, Ensign Ralph Osborn, succeeded single-handed in defeating a superior invading force during a mock battle. It was accomplished with the help of a pocket-sized submarine and a daring swim out of a torpedo tube by the hero.

The story was prophetic of the rise of the submarine. From 1895 to World War I, the submarine increased in length from 53 feet to 270 feet, in size from 73 tons to 270 tons, in speed from six knots to ten knots, in cruising range from 200 miles to 12,000 miles, in number of torpedos from one to ten. The first Holland boats took about 20 minutes to submerge. By the end of World War I, it was able to go under in three minutes.

In World War I, Germany at first had only 33 submarines and yet these few U-boats nearly succeeded in starving Britain into defeat. They sent down 13,000,000 tons of Allied shipping, including 349 British warships. Despite this impressive record, the U. S. Navy built an average of only three submarines a year between the two world wars. Battleships and carriers were everywhere considered as the true navy. At the beginning of World War II, the United States had only 57 submarines.

Ned Beach followed his father's footsteps in preparing himself for the Naval Academy at Annapolis. Equipped with a first rate mind, Ned attained top marks. He skipped grades with ease, loved to tinker with automobile engines, and devoured his father's popular books about life in Annapolis and on the sea. He idolized his father, who represented for him all that was finest in naval tradition.

Instead of attending a special preparatory school to ready himself for the Annapolis entrance examination, as most other applicants did, Ned simply collected a bunch of old examination papers. During his last year in high school, he studied them at night. It was the sort of self-discipline that was to remain with him in later years. He passed the exams, but he was only 16, too young to be admitted to Annapolis. He had to wait another year, and the exams then proved even easier for him.

His father's experiences in the Naval Academy were to prove invaluable to the son. The older Beach was a man of transparently honest character and of stubborn, rugged individualism. He had breathed the air of freedom in his youth in the wide-open spaces of Minnesota. His devout mother had taught him that faith in God moved mountains and that honesty was the only policy.

At first, everything about Navy rules and regulations had puzzled Ned's father. He could not understand how a chief petty officer could be both petty and chief. It seemed to him that the Navy was more concerned with cleanliness and polished shoes than with education. He kept bumping against Navy regulations, but he was saved by a good-natured disposition, and during World War I he rose to become the distinguished commanding officer of the battleship New York, then flagship of the American Battle Squadron in England. After his retirement, he became a professor at Stanford University and later, City Clerk and Assessor of the city of Palo Alto, California.

The father passed on his wisdom to his son. It enabled Ned Beach, who had the same independent streak as his father, to clear the rocks, shoals, and hazards of a multitude of Navy directions, instructions, and disciplines that reduced so drastically the number of graduates. His father taught him the necessity of learning to obey before learning how to command. His father impressed upon him that the privileges of officers were to be paid for by unfailing responsibility.

His father's advice was taken seriously by the young, handsome Annapolis midshipman. He buckled down to the study of mathematics, navigation, thermodynamics, electricity, and diesel engines. At the same time he never sacrificed friendship and understanding on the altar of technical studies.

The son made a remarkable record at the Naval Academy. He was Regimental Commander in his First Class year. On graduating he won the "Class of 1897" Sword as the man who had done the most "by his officer-like qualities and positive character to develop naval spirit and loyalty within the regiment." He graduated second of 581 in the class of 1939.

Ned Beach represented to his father a new generation of officers that would bring a new status to the U. S. Navy. No father could have been prouder on that graduation day. Twenty years later, Captain Beach wrote of this period: "The biggest driving force so far as I can identify it, for me, was the unfair deal Father received when his ship, USS Memphis, was wrecked in 1916. Actually, it was only 'unfair' in that the Navy always blames the unfortunate Captain, even though, as in Father's case, it was an 'Act of God' (a tidal wave), and he was technically exonerated. At the Naval Academy I resolved to 'make it up' for Father by making as good a record as I could . . . the biggest reward, for me, in my academic success . . . was the knowledge of the pleasure this gave him."

His father's advice to "stay with the big ships" induced the 22-year old ensign to select the cruiser Chester for his first ship. Ned Beach, however, had the stubborn individualism of his father, and he felt that he did not have enough to do.

The outbreak of war in Europe in 1939 brought a new directive stating that a number of old destroyers were to be taken out of "moth balls" and returned to duty. After three months on the Chester, Beach was transferred to the destroyer USS Lea, which happened to be exactly the same age as he. The change proved to be a lucky one for Ensign Beach. He found himself handling all kinds of varied duties—communication, torpedoes, gunnery, and the ship's tiny store. He was so busy that he did not have time to worry about having more to do. He soon realized that he had never been so completely happy.

The early success of the German U-boats in World

War II shook up Navy policy. Alfred T. Mahan, who had written a book on war strategy, proved to be correct. His theory was that national greatness and national commerce depended upon control of the sea lanes. The appalling number of ships sunk by the U-boats threatened the life line of raw materials which were absolutely necessary to keep the industrial machine of England going. The sinking of Allied ships had reached a rate that saw the Allies only a few months short of complete collapse. As U. S. entry into the war became more and more imminent, the U. S. Navy realized that submarines were sending more shipping to the bottom than all other agents of destruction combined.

There was now an urgent need for a vast number of smaller ships—for destroyers, escorts, and submarines. A hundred new submarines would have to be built overnight. This radical change in naval strategy struck home to Ensign Beach in September, 1941, when he and a number of other officers then serving in old destroyers were drafted into the submarine service.

During his two years in the Lea, young Beach had grown to love his old destroyer, and he was not pleased with his transfer. He knew the Lea, and he knew his job on board. Submarines had been farthest from his thoughts. They seemed to him skulking steel monsters of cold-blooded destruction.

Men who volunteered for submarine service in the early days of World War II were sometimes considered crackpots or suicidal. Most people felt a sense of horror about ocean depths. Life on a submarine, most Navy men thought, was like living in a mine shaft. Even the officers' quarters were no bigger than closets. Although famous officers like Admiral

Nimitz were witnesses to the contrary, many felt that nobody in his right mind would want to live such a life for the duration of the war.

To get more submariners, the Navy increased their pay 50 percent above normal. Even then Beach wanted to stay with his destroyer. But he had no choice. Most reluctantly, he left the USS Lea for the New London Submarine School.

Despite the urgent demand for men, it was not easy to qualify for submarines. The candidate who arrived at New London was carefully checked for eyesight, color perception, for near and far vision, for the ability to detect faint noises, and for the ability to discriminate the slightest difference in loudness and pitch of sound.

Each candidate was put through basic training in a submarine escape tank. He was scrutinized for his adaptability to all kinds of pressure changes. He was tested for any latent tendency toward panic in enclosed spaces. He went through all kinds of psychological tests. If he could not make up his mind quickly, if he could not make accurate decisions, if he were too excitable or erratic, he was not wanted in the submarine service.

Those who had not been eliminated went on to study the structure of submarines, the various piping and control systems, torpedo tubes, engines, and ship handling. A diving trainer was used which duplicated all the sensory impressions of the submarine as the student manipulated the plane controls and the controls for flooding, pumping, and blowing of water.

Eight weeks of study aboard a submarine followed. In the "school of the boat," the trainee learned to rig every compartment for diving, to man the controls for diving and surfacing, to fire torpedoes, and to operate the propulsion system.

Triton bored along smoothly in its true undersea element.

Beach went through this grueling training. His brain had to be razor-sharp and accurate. He had to know how to set the rudder just right, the trim just so. He had to learn to handle levers, knobs, and valves with the sure touch of a piano virtuoso.

He found himself enjoying the challenge. He realized that submariners were a special breed of men. They responded heroically to the lure and danger of the depths. There was a comradeship he had not known even in destroyers. The crew had to have absolute confidence in each other. They had to withstand extreme psychological strain without flaring up. Everyone had to know everything about a sub in case of an emergency. Rank had very little meaning, unless backed up with knowledge, experience, and confidence.

Within three months Beach had reached the top of his class at submarine school. He was promoted to lieutenant (j.g.) and was rushed to the Mare Island Navy Yard in California to join the USS *Trigger* which was under construction and was soon to be ready for service.

When he saw the *Trigger* for the first time, on the morning of New Year's Day, 1941, it was cluttered with hoses, ropes, tubes, and scraps of steel. His heart sank. It hardly looked like a fighting ship soon to enter the war zone.

At that time, the submarine was considered as a sort of scouting vessel, one which preceded the battleships and, more likely than not, was one of the first ships to be knocked off. The real slugging, Beach thought, would be done by the dreadnoughts, who would get all the glory. This fantasy blew up, suddenly, when the full news about Pearl Harbor became known.

There were no longer any dreadnoughts in the Pacific Fleet. Five waves of dive bombers and torpedo planes from six Japanese carriers had severely damaged all eight of the giant battleships at Pearl Harbor within one hour. Submarines, destroyers, and aircraft carriers would have to take the place of battleships. Like the young Spitfire pilots in the Battle of Britain, the young submariners found themselves flung into the front line of defense. Their assignment was to smash anything afloat that was Japanese. The *Trigger* was rushed to Pearl Harbor even before the training period was completed.

Beach saw with his own eyes the crushed backbone of the U. S. fleet. The *California* was half under water. The *Oklahoma* was completely upside-down, her huge belly and enormous bronze propellers sticking out of the scummy black oil covering the surface of the water in the harbor. The *West Virginia* was in dry-dock, a gaping hole in her side. Only the ruined masts of the *Arizona* were visible. And so it was with all the famous ships, whose pictures had hung on the walls of his room during his school days.

At this time the Japanese fleet was moving toward Midway Island, so the *Trigger* was hurried there, skipping the much-needed training at Pearl Harbor. The submarine made an overnight run to Midway, where it was to patrol two miles off shore. No sooner had she begun her patrol the next morning when *Trigger* ran head-on into a submerged coral wall. There she sat, stuck on a reef, a sitting duck for the invaders, who it was thought might make their first attempt to land that very day. It was a humiliating beginning.

A tug arrived at sunrise and the *Trigger* was pulled back into deep water. The invading fleet, however, never reached Midway. Admiral Fletcher and Admiral Spruance had caught it at sea the day before and Navy fliers had smashed most of the Japanese ships within a period of two minutes. The survivors scurried away in panic. It was a lucky day for the *Trigger*.

With the air-sea battle of Midway in June 1942, the Navy began to fight its way back across the Pacific. War in the Pacific became the greatest naval war the world had ever seen, and the submarine branch became one of the most important arms of the Navy. Representing only 1.6 percent of U. S. Naval strength, it accounted for 63 percent of all enemy shipping which was sunk.

By the end of 1943, Japan was unable to bring in enough coal and steel to make up her losses. They were losing 26 ships for every American sub that went down. By May 1944, the whole South China Sea had become unsafe for Japanese shipping. Another six months and the total Japanese merchant marine had fallen to less than 2,-000,000 tons—1,000,000 less than necessary to maintain prewar civilian economy. By the end of the war, the Japanese had lost 1,150 merchant ships, three carriers, four escort carriers, one battleship, one cruiser and about half the Japanese destroyer service under the deluge of American submarine torpedoes.

The *Trigger* played an honored role in that far-flung battle. Beach, ultimately her Executive Officer, survived the ordeal of a dozen patrols, knocking out more than 40 ships, including a giant aircraft carrier. His heroism won him the Navy Cross, two Silver Stars, two Bronze Stars and the ribbons of the Presidential Unit Citations awarded to the *Trigger* and *Tirante*, on which Beach later also served as Executive Officer. At the age of 27, he was rewarded with the command of his own ship, the *Piper*.

The World War II years were the most concentrated years of his life, an ordeal of fire which forged his character to steel-like maturity. Few submariners who had seen as much action as he had, survived to tell about it. In all, 374 officers and 3,131 enlisted men went down with more than 50 American submarines.

Young Beach had entered the war fresh from Annapolis, fun-loving, and good-natured. He emerged a tough-minded, battle-hardened man. The cruel experience, however, had made him fall in love with the "silent service." After the war he called the submarine "the most beautiful and responsive creature I had ever known."

Numerically, the Japanese submarines were equal to the Americans. Then why had they been beaten so badly? Beach pondered the enigma after the war, and could come up with only one answer.

He knew that American submariners were not more fearless than the Japanese, and that the enemy submarines were good ships. He felt that the answer must lie in the difference in the manner of thinking between the Japanese and the Americans. The Japanese military caste indoctrinated the nation into a mental rigidity that knew only the robot reaction of strict obedience to orders. Thus the Japanese were incapable of initiative in times of crisis.

When the Japanese military clique saw everything collapsing, they threw their best trained warriors into certain and useless death. In their rigid view, refusal to admit defeat insured victory. They sacrificed irreplaceable skill in an empty gesture of heroism, whether it had any strategic importance or not. As the Americans advanced from island to island, the robot-minded Japanese army leaders, who controlled naval operations as well as the government, could think of no better use for their own subs than to carry rice to beleaguered garrisons on islands that were of no further use to them, and in many cases were later to be bypassed by General MacArthur.

When *Tirante* tried to rescue some flyers from a Japanese plane downed in the China Sea, one of them threw a lighted aircraft flare at the *Tirante* in a pathetic gesture of defiance. Then they jumped from the plane into the sea to avoid capture. One flier ducked out of his life jacket, swam away, swallowed water, and sank. A second willingly climbed aboard the sub. The man who had thrown the flare then allowed himself to be dragged aboard, pretending to have fainted in order to save face. He had not the nerve to carry out his own suicide order, though one of his men did. Such were the twisted personalities created by a heartless military dictatorship.

Beach and his fellow submariners shuddered to think of a world ruled by such fanaticism. Against such spiritual darkness, democracy shone with a more resplendent light.

Chapter *3*

Beach and Rickover

By this time a lieutenant commander in rank, Beach first heard of the atom bomb when he backed the *Piper* away from its berth at Apra Harbor, Guam, on August 5, 1945. He was moving out toward the Sea of Japan, to what he knew would be his last war patrol, when the radio suddenly announced that a new and terrible bomb had been dropped on Hiroshima. Uranium had been made to give up a tiny fraction of its atomic energy; yet that little fraction was enough to flatten a city. Beach could not conceive then what a fateful role atomic energy would play in his life.

After the war, Beach reported to the Navy Department in Washington, D. C., where he was first aide to the Chief of Naval Personnel, and later was appointed to the office of the Chief of Naval Operations, where he was given a desk job in the Navy's new Atomic Defense Section.

Lieutenant Commander Beach first met Captain Hyman G. Rickover in 1947. Beach was 29 years old, and Rickover was 20 years his senior. Rickover was obsessed with the "crackpot" idea that an atomic submarine could actually be built. His one-man crusade to push the Navy into the nuclear age had just begun. The role of a gadfly buzzing angrily at those in authority is never popular, and Rickover was not a popular man.

Beach, by way of contrast, was one of the most popular young submarine officers in the Navy. For his achievements in the Pacific war he was entitled to wear as many as 15 of the nation's most distinguished medals and ribbons. In Rickover's judgment, Beach was definitely the best man to get a certain letter cleared through the chain of command.

The letter was addressed to the Secretary of the Navy, and it would have to be signed by the Navy's top Admiral, Chester Nimitz. In order to get Nimitz to sign it, it would have to be cleared and endorsed by other ranking admirals. The Nimitz signature in turn would convince the Secretary of the Navy.

It was a strong letter detailing the reasons why an atomic submarine was a military necessity. The 29-year old naval hero instantly realized the importance of nuclear power to submarines. But getting Navy approval was no easy task because atomic energy, at that time, was so little understood. During the war, censorship on matters concerning atomic research had been complete. There was not a news item, article, or book on the subject. There was profound ignorance about it everywhere. Atomic energy was still something suspect, fearful, and strange.

Rickover, even then, was noted for having one of the most learned scientific and engineering backgrounds in the Navy. His rise in the U. S. Navy was distinguished. He was born of a poor immigrant Jewish family who could not offer their son an education, so he took and won a competi-

Captain Beach at one of the Triton's periscopes

tive examination for appointment to the Naval Academy in Annapolis. After cramming and passing his second hurdle, the entrance examinations, Rickover became ill with diphtheria in his first year at the Academy. To catch up on his studies, he worked late into the night despite regulations. One failure in exams might mean dismissal.

That terrible first year of self-discipline led him to prefer study to social life. He learned to enjoy the pursuit of knowledge for its own sake.

He revealed his remarkable grasp of electrical and engineering knowledge three years after graduation by installing a complex 500-unit battle telephone system on the battleship Nevada. Later, when he became an engineering officer in a submarine, he preferred to handle all the repair work himself instead of asking for a Navy-yard repair job.

When he became Inspector of Naval Material at Philadelphia, he insisted that private industry redesign the machines they sold to the Navy. When he was second-in-command of the electrical section of the Bureau of Ships, all electrical equipment had to meet his specifications to make them more battleworthy. At one time he pushed through a $12,000,000 order for electric cables to explode mines, despite English patent rights and a lack of official Navy permission. The cables were an outstanding success. Instead of being punished for insubordination, he was praised for his initiative and foresight. The same thing happened with Rickover's insistence on a new infrared signaling and detection device, which made possible invisible communication at night.

During World War II, he traveled 100,000 miles a year to inspect every damaged warship. He insisted that the smashed battleships in Pearl Harbor be repaired on the spot instead of being towed to Navy yards on the mainland. He rewrote catalogs of tens of thousands of parts to eliminate duplication and waste. At the end of the war, he cleaned out and cocooned the ships on the West Coast in record time on a production line basis.

His Navy career was devoted to changing, simplifying, improving practically all mechanisms that met his roving eye. To do so he had to be a whip to others. It meant 16-hour days, long harangues to explain and to educate, and unabashed tongue lashings of superiors or inferiors who lacked his engineering knowledge. He escaped punishment over and over again only because of the reputation he built as a man who got things done.

When Admiral Earle Mills assigned him to study atomic fission in Oak Ridge, a sixth sense compelled Captain Rickover to look into some secret files in the Bureau of Ships. Six different reports advocating atomic-powered ships had been filed away.

Most fascinating of the papers was that of Dr. Phil Abelson on how the Navy might build an atomic-powered sub. Water could be pumped under great pressure through pipes within an atomic reactor core, said Abelson. The tremendous heat of fission could raise the temperature of the pressurized water to any desired temperature without converting it to steam. The heat in the pressurized water could be transferred to a separate piping system where water under less pressure would be changed to steam without becoming radioactive. The steam could then be used to turn standard turbines and propellers.

Here was a practical method that started Rickover thinking. A mere engineering problem stood in the way of a project that could revolutionize the Navy—if they had the wisdom to see it. As it turned out, for a period of two years, Rickover and three associates had the field all to themselves. No one else wanted anything to do with an engine that was pronounced dangerous and impractical, if not downright crazy.

Rickover knew from the beginning that he had an epoch-making idea. The burning of coal converts only a

[43]

third of a billionth of its original mass into heat; the splitting atom converts three million times that amount into heat. Simply put, one pound of uranium could produce as much heat as the burning of 2,500,000 tons of coal. Rickover never lost the flush of ecstasy he had when he first glimpsed the magic potential of an atomic engine.

Few people, then, shared his enthusiasm. The prevailing emphasis among the scientists at Oak Ridge was either on building better bombs or on finding a means of producing electric power from atomic fission on an experimental basis. No one was interested in making a practical atomic engine. Ironically, Rickover's engine was destined to be the first to produce electric power, but, at that time, no one was in a hurry except Rickover.

Rickover made a tour of U. S. atomic installations, trying to get the backing of the great atomic scientists— Oppenheimer, Fermi, Teller—for his atomic submarine idea. Teller was the only one who helped. He wrote a letter to Dr. Lawrence R. Hafstad, who headed a committee on defense research. Teller strongly urged that Rickover's group should get a first model in working order within a short time. He said Rickover and his assistants were specialists in high-pressure steam, and they would not be in competition with the physicists. Bold engineering projects proved very useful in World War II and they should be continued.

Teller's letter, which was to prove so fateful later on, brought no immediate results. Atomic work, aside from bombs, was practically at a standstill after the war. Physicists were too deeply involved in theoretical research to think of practical projects. The idea of an atomic submarine became so remote that Rickover's group was disbanded. Rickover, himself, became a sort of consultant on nuclear matters to Admiral Mills, marking time until he would be needed.

He found himself with no special duties. He had reached an impasse—without title, without money, without authority, with nothing to look forward to. Many men in his position would have resigned from the Navy and taken a high paying engineering position in civilian life.

Suddenly, out of a clear sky, the Atomic Energy Commission (AEC) revealed the first twinge of interest. It asked the Bureau of Ships to formulate a report on the Navy's theories about atomic propulsion of ships. Rickover postponed an operation in a hospital to write a detailed report flatly stating that an atomic power reactor employing water as the cooling medium was 95 percent ready to be built into a submarine.

Months later the AEC gave a $2,250,000 contract to General Electric to work on a heat-transfer unit. Rickover was allotted $30,000 to continue research on his atomic submarine engine. To Rickover, the AEC decision was a tragic waste of time, money, and organization. He felt an engine should be developed as a whole. Rickover, therefore, deviated from his instructions. He used the $30,000 to have his former group at Oak Ridge design a complete atomic propulsion system. At least somebody would be working on a submarine engine, even if only a few blueprints resulted.

With blueprints in his hands, Rickover was ready for his next move. He would try to get Admiral Nimitz and the

Secretary of the Navy to back him up. But first, he would have to make a convert of a prominent submariner. This was where Beach entered the picture.

Beach was greatly impressed with this straightforward naval engineer with so brilliant a background. Rickover knew his statements sounded incredulous, so he sought to reassure Beach that he knew what he was talking about.

Atomic reactors already in existence contained all the ingredients for an efficient submarine engine, Rickover said. There was, first of all, the nuclear fuel that was, at last, in plentiful supply. The reactors themselves could be made to fit into a submarine. The fantastic heat of the reactors could be drawn off by water piped into the core. The cooling pipes would prevent the core from melting down. Control mechanisms for starting, slowing down, or blanking out the "atomic fire" were common knowledge. The atomic sub engine, in short, was only a matter of assembling elements already available.

The gleam in Rickover's eyes was bright. His engine could launch the thousand ships of a new Navy. It was as real to him as to be almost within his grasp. Get a grapefruit-sized piece of U-235 "cooking," push some cadmium or graphite rods in and out, add a closed system of pressurized water, bring a heat exchanger next to it, and there was the steam, freed from radioactivity, available for years at a time to whirl the turbines and turn the propellers of a submarine. And this engine would never need air or oxygen at any point in the cycle.

Rickover's enthusiasm was contagious. His plan was

simple enough for anyone to understand, or so it seemed to Beach as he made the rounds of admirals with the exciting idea. They turned him down cold. Their arguments, spoken in tones of icy calculation, had down-to-earth wisdom and common sense.

How could twelve feet of heavy shielding necessary for an atomic reactor fit into the tiny space of a submarine? Where was the metal piping that would not disintegrate under constant nuclear bombardment? The pressurized water in its closed cycle was bound to build up radioactive contamination over a period of time. There was no guarantee that the concentrated Uranium-235 reacting for months, would not suddenly get out of control and become a deadly atomic bomb.

Then again, how could one make repairs in a radioactive engine? Certainly, no hand could be thrust in. The atomic engine for a submarine or any ship, in their words, was "technically premature."

Crestfallen, Beach reported back to Rickover. When he heard their arguments, Rickover snorted with disdain. They were repeating arguments that professional engineers would dismiss with contempt. Any broadly educated scientific man knew that an atomic pile could never be a bomb, Rickover declared. At worst a runaway reactor would only melt the core. Submarines could be made wider and bigger to accommodate the heavy shielding. Stronger metals for pipes could be fabricated to resist radioactivity. Their arguments proved they had no genuine engineering knowledge.

Rickover went further. He claimed their attitude was dangerous to the safety of the country. Had they forgotten the role played by submarines in the last two wars? Germany had almost won two world wars with its submarines. At one time, in 1917, the British forces in France had supplies left for only four days. U. S. submarines might have licked Japan singlehanded in World War II. Napoleon and Hitler very nearly conquered the world, but failed because they could not control the seas. Surely, the admirals were aware that the Soviet Union was building submarines at a rapid rate. There could be only one reason. In a few years they intended to be able to control the seas.

There was no time to delay. The admirals opposing him were displaying a "convoy" mind. They were prepared to go only as fast as the slowest ship of a convoy. With that sort of speed, said Rickover, the atomic bomb would never have been realized.

It would take time, of course, to build an atomic sub. It previously took five years to build a destroyer. If the Navy were to pull all stops and push ahead as it did during World War II an atomic sub could be built in the same time it took to build a destroyer.

The Navy should have pushed ahead with the atomic sub right after the war, Rickover insisted. Two years had been lost already. The word, "impossible," did not exist in Rickover's dictionary. He had the unshakeable faith of a firm believer. Those who heard him could not help but believe with him.

Beach, himself, had no difficulty in seeing the point. He was only too aware of the difference an atomic submarine would make. He had only to recall the limitations of his subs during the war. Hundreds of men he had known had died because their subs were not fast enough or could not stay submerged long enough.

Beach remembered having to surface every night to start the diesel engines and recharge the batteries. The recharging sometimes took as long as nine hours, enough for enemy sonar and radar to track him down. In battle areas, he had to come to the surface within sight of the mainland of Japan. Even if he stayed down, creeping along, his ship could cover only 100 miles in an entire 24 hours—and by then it *had* to come up, for its batteries would be exhausted.

Frequently, his sub had been cornered by enemy destroyers. He always faced the same cruel dilemma. If he ran off at high speed, his batteries might be exhausted in less than an hour. If the sonar operators of the enemy ship could locate him, he would be a sure target for depth charges. If he went slower, the batteries would last longer, but there was even less chance of getting away. Two hundred feet down, a mere tap from a nearby depth charge might add enough extra weight to the tremendous water pressure to buckle some plates of the sub's hull, and that would spell the end.

These problems would disappear with an atomic sub. There would be no worry about battery power. The atomic sub, streamlined like a fish, could speed away at great depths and at great speed. It would not be dependent on frequent operation of the battery recharging equipment. With no need for air to run the engines, it could stay down, and run at high speed as long as there was air enough inside the sub for the crew to breathe.

[49]

Such a ship was worth fighting for. Beach even wrote a short story under a fictitious name describing the havoc one atomic sub could inflict on enemy vessels. He spoke up constantly to his superiors and finally he began to notice a shift in attitude within the Pentagon. Enough admirals were finally persuaded to clear the letter composed by Rickover.

In some high Navy circles the atomic submarine had become a military necessity. Admiral Nimitz signed the letter promptly and gladly. It was endorsed by the Secretary of the Navy. It was sent to the AEC. Months went by. Nothing happened. Rickover placed a blank piece of paper in a folder titled "Atomic Naval Propulsion." That was all he had to show in his semi-annual report.

Beach, however, did not give up hope. He knew that the Navy would have an atomic submarine sooner or later. He went out to Oak Ridge for an indoctrination period under Rickover. He persuaded two friends to transfer to his section, where they could begin studying the new field of atomic physics. There was a sure future, he told them, in atomic submarines. One friend, Lieutenant Commander E. P. Wilkinson (Dennis for short) was later to become the first skipper of the *Nautilus*.

Chapter *4*

Period of Transition

After thirty months ashore, Beach was scheduled for rotation to sea duty. He actually yearned for the sea. Whatever agitation was in him would be soothed with the calm of the undersea world. The routine of sea life—its order and punctuality—liberated his imagination. The sea, somehow, as it does for all true sailors, made him feel free.

He was offered the command of the *Amberjack*—the very latest type of submarine with a snorkel device. The snorkel was a telescopic pipe, capable of sucking in air, while the submarine was submerged to periscope depth. This steady supply of air, feeding the diesel engines, permitted the sub to run submerged for weeks at a time. For the first time in the history of the U. S. Navy, a submarine could breathe without coming completely to the surface.

The design of this latest model sub was also changed. Though her main, or "pressure" hull was not affected, her entire superstructure was extensively streamlined. The *Amberjack* was the fastest, most maneuverable ship Beach had ever served in.

Changes were taking place in the entire U. S. Navy. Battleships were no longer built. Beach remembered the battleships his father commanded, monsters that had to be huge and heavy to absorb the earthquake recoil of their massive guns, to carry the heavy armor that enabled them to withstand punishment. Air power had been the Navy's strongest weapon in World War II, and the aircraft carrier had taken the battleship's place in America's battle line.

An age of specialization was setting in, too. Radar pickets, as an example, had relatively few armaments, but they were loaded with more detection equipment than any ship ever had before. Their mission was to help detect enemy aircraft.

More escort carriers were being built. Escort carriers developed near the end of World War II had put aircraft into the middle of the ocean to detect German submarines, radio their location, and attack them. Attack carriers had supported the sea and land campaigns against the Japanese Navy, its conquests, and eventually against Japan itself.

Escort destroyers were now outfitted with the most modern anti-submarine equipment. They could throw out salvos of rocket-propelled anti-submarine bombs. These "hedgehogs," as they were called, did not explode unless they actually hit a submarine. When they hit, the submarine was always seriously damaged, in most cases sunk. Thus, they were superior to depth charges because they did not interfere with the searching sonar equipment, which had been constantly disturbed by the explosions of depth charges.

Submarines, too, were becoming specialized. The Navy had begun experimenting with submarines with such special functions as laying mines, carrying oil and supplies, detecting and attacking enemy subs, or acting as a submersible radar picket.

While he commanded the *Amberjack*, Beach had much to do with the development of new submarine tactics. After an all-too-short period, he was ordered back to a desk job in Washington at the end of August, 1949. This time he became Naval assistant to the newly created Chairman of the Joint Chiefs of Staff, General Omar Bradley. A few months earlier he had become a commander in the Navy.

While Beach had been away at sea, Rickover continued his one-man battle for the atomic submarine. Always alert for any opportunity to advance his cause, he pounced on a notice of an annual meeting of the Symposium on Undersea Warfare. An influential group of men would be assembled. Rickover wrote a speech and persuaded Admiral Mills to read it at the Symposium. It was an attack that jolted the Atomic Energy Commission.

After this slam-bang speech, the situation started to change. The Committee on Undersea Warfare openly approved construction of a nuclear submarine. The Joint Chiefs of Staff officially endorsed it. Everything that Beach had so vainly attempted to do for Rickover became suddenly an accomplished fact. Overnight, the entire Navy brass seemed to accept the idea of a nuclear submarine. On August 4, 1948, Admiral Mills chose Rickover to organize a nuclear power division within the Navy's Bureau of Ships.

Rickover then served notice on the AEC in a letter signed by Admiral Mills that if the AEC did not act on an atomic powered ship, the Navy would be forced to do it alone. Lawrence R. Hafstad, who was in charge of the AEC's Department of Reactor Development, recalled the letter concerning Rickover sent to him by Teller the year before. To resolve the problem Hafstad now formed, finally, a Naval Reactor Branch in the AEC. Rickover was put in charge.

By August 19, 1949, Rickover found himself in an extraordinary position. He had created for himself two executive positions, one in the Bureau of Ships and another in the AEC. In both organizations, he was placed in complete charge of the development of atomic reactors for naval vessels. Now, all he needed was money.

Fate showered him suddenly with more blessings than he had ever dreamed of. The tension in Korea resulted in a $2,000,000,000 naval appropriation bill getting through Congress. Funds were included in the bill for a new submarine that was to be propelled by nuclear power. Rickover had $3,000,000 to begin operations.

Here was a coup almost without precedent in the history of the Navy. One man with a new idea was given the chance to develop it with almost limitless funds. Rickover had boasted over and over again that he could build an atomic submarine in five years. Now he would have to make good on his boast.

For the next few years, Rickover maintained a round-the-clock schedule. He would be in his office at 8 a. m. and leave at 4 p.m., more likely than not to take a plane to an atomic center in a different part of the country. He would return on an overnight sleeper and be back at his desk in Washington the following morning.

There were no textbooks, no rules, no precedents to

follow. Everything had to be done by trial and error. Fortunately, decisions were his alone to make. There was no clutter of a chain of command to delay matters. Rickover, in fact, had almost the power of a dictator, and he needed it to get a ten-year project done in half that time.

One of the first things he did with his new authority was to get Westinghouse into the atomic energy business. He persuaded the company to concentrate on a complete atomic reactor system instead of merely a heat-exchange apparatus. A mechanism, he told the Westinghouse engineers, should be tackled from the beginning as a system and designed as a whole.

He came up with a daring idea. Build two atomic propulsion systems of the same size and at approximately the same time. Westinghouse was to build one atomic engine inside a submarine hull on dry land. The Electric Boat Company at Groton, Connecticut, would build the seagoing duplicate. A time schedule was set up so that the duplicate would lag slightly behind the original. Any changes or improvements could thus be quickly adopted in the seagoing copy. The land-based model was named Mark I— the duplicate, Mark II.

The creation of the first reactor system went on in an eight-story high hangar with six emergency ventilators in the roof. The reactor compartment and engine rooms of a submarine were constructed with the reactor room contained in a 50-foot tank of water. The reactor system consisted of the reactor, shielding, piping, heat exchangers, and pumps. The steam turbines that would drive two ship's propellers were located farther aft, in the engine rooms. The system would be tested as nearly as possible under the same conditions an actual submarine would encounter at sea.

At one stage in the development, Westinghouse wanted to spread out parts all over the building so that engineers could experiment with each one separately and then have them assembled later. Rickover insisted upon the assembled version first, calculating that he could save two years of time that way.

The deadline was constantly in his mind. There was no time to waste.

For reasons of safety, it was decided that the location of the Mark I would be on a 400,000-acre isolated site in the desert regions of the Snake River in Idaho. Since it was to be the world's first nuclear power plant, no one could guarantee that an explosion might not take place.

A power reactor is a tremendously concentrated source of energy. If not controlled, it can produce heat fast enough to reach 10,000-degrees Fahrenheit. There was always the danger of a meltdown of the core or of a steam explosion. The possibility of an atomic explosion was convincingly eradicated, but of course the uninitiated feared this also. Eighty different kinds of controls were worked out so as to "scram" (shut down) the reactor within a fraction of a second.

Shielding the reactor presented a special problem. The engineers could not use the heavy, concrete blockhouses that were in use at Oak Ridge and Hanford. The shielding had to be lighter, small enough to fit into a submarine, and obviously more efficient. The engineers calculated that a few feet of metal shielding of various types would keep the radiation at a safe level. But only final testing would prove that answer.

The heat-transfer system was another calculated risk. Would the metal barrier between the two piping systems allow heat but not radioactivity to pass through?

While Rickover was struggling with his problems, Beach found the time to write his epic stories of the submariners of World War II. Writing these stories of the men of the "silent service" was a sacred duty to him. As a submariner, he knew what it was to be trapped within a submarine listening to depth charges explode one after another. He knew what doomed men endured in their last agony.

Even as he was writing the true stories that would later comprise his bestseller *Submarine*, he kept asking himself, "Why had these men died and not myself?" Was he more alert? Did he have a better crew—a better ship? In final analysis the submarine, itself, was the key. The submarines of World War II had a fatal weakness—low endurance while submerged. Once a really good anti-submarine team got after them, escape was difficult, especially if the subs' batteries were already partly exhausted, as of course they would be if they had just made an attack. Improved weapons and better detection equipment were bound to make survival more difficult in the future. Development of a *true* submarine, the one all submariners had been dreaming of, was now vital.

For this reason, he was grateful for a man like Rickover, who had dedicated himself to build the submarine of the

[57]

future. If Rickover were successful in building his under-water dream boat, then the sacrifice of submariners might not have to be repeated.

Most of the stories in Beach's book dealt with the exploits of his own submarine—*Trigger*—on which he had served as Diving Officer, Engineer, and finally as Executive Officer. He had been transferred to another submarine just before the *Trigger* went on its last, fatal war patrol. He would be haunted forever by the faces of shipmates he would never see again.

When Beach heard that a new high-speed submarine was being built at Groton, Connecticut and that its name would be *Trigger*, something flipped in his heart. He had a teriffic compulsion to take command of the new submarine by that name. He asked for and received assignment as its Prospective Commanding Officer. The new *Trigger* took a year longer to complete. She was commissioned on March 31, 1952, at which time Beach assumed full command.

Not many months later, the newspapers were full of exciting reports about the start of construction of the first nuclear powered submarine, the *Nautilus*. Beach's friend, Dennis Wilkinson, was to become her skipper. Wilkinson had studied to be a professor of mathematics before the war, and had begun the study of atomic energy at Beach's own suggestion.

The glowing press accounts of the future of the *Nautilus* made things difficult for Rickover. No one seemed to suspect that endless problems still faced him before the ship could become a reality. He realized with dismay that there simply was not enough exact scientific knowledge about atomic energy to avoid the time-consuming delays of trial and error.

The engineers met their first big headache when they tested steel under neutron bombardment. The steel simply fell apart. Then they tested all kinds of metals to see if some other would be more resistant. The results were disconcerting. Only one metal, zirconium, stood up against the neutrons, but it was so rare that not even twenty pounds of it could be found in the United States. Its cost was something like $450,000 a pound.

Since the word "impossible" did not exist for Rickover, he demanded that Westinghouse go into large scale production of the metal to lower its price. Metals like zirconium and hafnium, he said, were destined to be the metals of the future. By this time Westinghouse realized that Rickover spoke for the U. S. government. They needed no further persuasion. Westinghouse went into a new kind of business—the manufacture of corrosion-resistant metals.

With problems piling up, Rickover needed engineers who were gifted with the imagination to tackle them. He interviewed more than 1,000 men, but almost all of them understood only the routine procedures taught them in college. In the end, Rickover decided to create a special nuclear engineering school under his direction. It was the only way he could see to encourage a new type of thinking.

Original thinking was needed to solve the new problems that were arising. For example, all the moving parts of the reactor had to be lubricated by hot radioactive water instead of oil. This was something new. Electric motors had to be built that would run under water. Gadgets had to be inserted that would count the neutrons shooting out of the reactor core. Pumps would have to be placed inside pipes to circulate pressurized water and they would have to be leakproof. The entire system would have to be designed in such a way as rarely, if ever, to need repair.

The only possible solution to the repair problem was to provide standbys in duplicate or triplicate. If one part failed, another part could take over automatically. Designers concentrated on closed, automatic systems.

Completed portions of the reactor system had to undergo severe shock treatment. They were placed in specially built submarines, 50 feet long, with miniature machinery propelling them into Chesapeake Bay. They were submerged and blasted with "baby" depth charges. Delicate meters, controls, and electrical equipment proved to be the most vulnerable. They had to be rebuilt and made battleproof.

A World War II sub was scheduled to be severely depth-charged for experimental purposes. Seven of its compartments were filled with components of the atomic engine. Movie films revealed which pieces failed to function. These pieces were sent back to the manufacturers with a stern demand that they be made shockproof. Rickover was trying to create a submarine that would be able to continue operations after enemy depth charges had exploded just outside the hull.

At the keel-laying ceremony of the *Nautilus* on June 14, 1952, President Harry S. Truman prophesied, "The engine of the *Nautilus* will have as revolutionary an effect on the navies of the world as did the first ocean-going steamship of 120 years ago."

This was spoken at a time when Rickover and his engineers were not sure whether their atomic reactor system would work. The big question still remained whether valves, pumps, and control-rod mechanisms would continue to operate for long periods. Perhaps the entire system would work for only a few hours. If so, it would prove to be no better than the electric storage batteries already installed in all submarines. There was still a year's work to be done before the final test could be made. The final test, however, would take place within the five-year deadline Rickover had set himself.

Chapter *5*

Rickover's Triumph

While Rickover and the engineers were rushing to complete the atomic engine of the *Nautilus*, the U. S. Navy was heavily engaged in the Korean War. It sent five tons of supplies for each man who went to Korea, and it sent 64 pounds of supplies a day to keep him fighting. The Navy was to take 76,000,000 tons of cargo and 5,000,000 passengers to the Korean area.

To be able to get into the fighting as quickly as possible, Beach speeded up the shakedown program of the new *Trigger*. During a sea test, he pushed the engines to their top speed against 20-feet waves. Suddenly the engines began to shudder. A piece of propeller had broken off. As the *Trigger* returned to drydock back in New London, the skipper was depressed about the breakdown. Perhaps he had been too impatient, too harsh with the brand-new submarine. The *Trigger* was not the supership Beach had hoped it to be. The foolproof submarine would have to wait for Rickover.

While he was standing on the deck of the *Trigger* as it was being nudged into dry dock, the arm of a huge crane swooped down on Beach, practically handing him a telephone. Washington was on the line, and he was ordered to report at once.

On the way to Washington, he wondered if he were to be put on the carpet for the broken propeller. But it was hardly possible that Washington could have heard about the accident so quickly. More likely, he suspected, he might have to face a grilling about his book *Submarine*. He had written about faulty torpedos and other difficulties as honestly as he could. Perhaps too honestly! Or perhaps it might be that some security officer had found fault with his short story about an atomic sub which a popular magazine had recently published. Whatever it was, the urgent phone call meant that something pretty big was brewing.

When he reached Washington he was told that the incoming President Dwight D. Eisenhower had appointed him as his naval aide. Beach was completely flabbergasted. A few months later at his desk in the White House he learned the secret details of the final test of the Mark I, the forerunner of the reactor system which would be installed in the *Nautilus*.

The final test was to determine how much power could be generated by the Mark I, and how long the system could run. The Navy and the AEC had already spent $250,000,000 on a project whose success was still to be proved. Rickover and AEC representatives arrived for the final test on May 31, 1953.

The switch was thrown by Commissioner Murray. Men anxiously watched instruments. The atoms were obedient. The chain reaction was throwing off the anticipated amount of heat. The metal shielding was preventing radioactivity from escaping from the reactor. Steam was being produced and was whirling the turbine blades. Everything seemed to register according to plan. After a two-hour run, during which power levels of several thousand horsepower were reached, the reactor was shut down.

So far, so good. Everybody was smiling. More critical tests were tried out in the following weeks, and the power level was cautiously and gradually increased. It was necessary to be sure that at higher temperatures there would be equally positive control of the reactor.

As power was gradually raised, there was a constant plague of "scrams." There were 80 automatic instruments which slowed down or shut down the reactor if the power raced too high. These automatic safety circuits were causing the reactor to shut down too frequently. The number of safety devices was gradually reduced from 80 to 20, and their reliability improved. One rule was paramount: with safety and efficiency there would be no compromise.

Fortunately, the radiation levels proved to be less than half of what had been expected. The lead metal walls provided complete safety.

At last, Mark I was scheduled to be run for a period of two days at maximum power. Towards the end of this 48-hour test, Rickover made a dramatic decision. Keep the engine running at full speed until it made an imaginary trip across the Atlantic, he ordered. A map was posted on a wall and a line was drawn from Nova Scotia to Ireland. The engine was to run at a speed of 20 knots, and the "distance" covered every 24 hours was to be marked off.

[65]

No submarine had ever run submerged at top speed for more than 20 miles. To cross the Atlantic at top speed was an incredible challenge for a brand-new engine. Beach recalled his broken propeller when he heard about this decision.

Some of the engineers raised anguished cries of protest. Mark I would be ruined! But Rickover insisted and agreed to take the sole responsibility.

It was the most fateful decision of his life. Failure could mean the ruin of his career in the Navy. The Navy Selection Board had already twice "passed over" Captain Rickover for promotion to Rear Admiral. Any Naval Captain who was "passed over" for the second time was expected to resign. But an exception had been made in Rickover's case. There had been a public clamor against his being forced to resign. There was to be a third hearing by the Selection Board. Their decision was to come in a matter of days. Failure of Mark I would mean a third rejection, and Rickover's usefulness to the Navy would be ended forever.

It became clear to Beach, who followed the Rickover case closely, that Rickover was more interested in the success of the atomic submarine than in his own career. The new submarine had become to him a symbol of the new age of technology and the future of the United States as the leading nation on earth.

Rickover's theories were well known to Beach. According to Rickover, that nation would survive that could improve its technology to keep pace with its population. In his arguments he used China as an example. At the time of Marco Polo, the Chinese were the greatest civilization on earth. But China failed to keep technological pace with the needs of its rapidly increasing population. When its population reached hundreds of millions, China sank to the lowest subsistence level of any nation on earth.

The United States was threatened with a parallel situation. In just 40 years the United States would have a population equal to the present population of India. To maintain its present standard of living, the United States would have need of all the engineering help it could get—as many as one engineer for every 20 citizens of its population. It would need enormous amounts of atomic energy. Therefore, Mark I could be a turning point in the history of the nation. If Mark I were successful, it would mean 'that a new technological age had begun.

Rickover's order that the Mark I make a full-power, imaginary trip across the Atlantic was obeyed. At the end of 48 hours it was running smoothly, but by the 60th hour, difficulties began to develop. Carbon dust was being deposited on windings of armatures. The instruments measuring radioactivity became erratic. One of the pumps developed a whining sound.

The men observing the operation began to worry, but Rickover saw no major hazard. The engineering crew took heart at his courage and worked all the harder to repair what could be repaired while the engine was running.

Finally, the marks on the chart revealed the end of the imaginary non-stop Atlantic crossing. Later, when inspection was made of the inside of the atomic core, the engineers were astounded to find no "poisoning" of the core, no defects of any kind. As far as the atomic heart of the engine was concerned, Mark I could have circumnavigated the world. Rickover was vindicated. A few days after the "Atlantic crossing," he was informed that the Selection Board had selected him for promotion to rear admiral.

Beach served at the White House during the first four years of the Eisenhower Administration. The sea kept tugging at his heart and he poured it out in his writing. He published his novel *Run Silent, Run Deep* in 1955. This book was written between 1953 and 1955, mostly at home late at night and early in the morning. "After a year I had laboriously got half way through; then I asked for two weeks leave and finished the job in ten days of concentration," Beach reported. He had produced another bestseller, and this time Hollywood was interested. Beach saw his characters transferred to the screen in portrayals by Clark Gable, Burt Lancaster, and others.

Four years ashore seemed a long time to Beach. He felt he "was marking time while the Navy moved along." He had been promoted to the rank of captain, which entitled him to supervise a division of four destroyers or to command a deep-draft ship of more than 20,000 tons. Eisenhower let him go at the end of the President's first term.

Beach could now be considered to be on the road toward the rank of rear admiral. But admiral stripes are usually given only to an officer who has a background of combat and deep-draft commands. Perhaps Navy headquarters had this in mind when Beach was offered the command of the 30,000-ton fleet-oiler *USS Salamonie*.

Captain Beach found it a full-time job to make the rusty old *Salamonie* as spick and span as a submarine. Her decks and hull were cleared of rust and covered with red lead so thoroughly that Captain Beach heard himself nick-named "Red Lead Ned." Through many months in 1957, the *Salamonie* lumbered through the Atlantic and the Mediterranean refueling ships of the line.

On the way back from the Mediterranean late in December, 1957, the *Salamonie* received a distress signal from a group of three destroyers that were being bounced about in a raging Atlantic storm. They were nearly out of fuel when the *Salamonie* arrived, and 30-foot waves made hose connections impossible. Nevertheless, they tried, because it was the only thing to do. One of the destroyers rammed the *Salamonie* and holed her stern. Part of the destroyer's deck was smashed.

The destroyer's skipper radioed it might be advisable to abandon ship. Beach responded with the stern rejoinder that no ship of the U. S. Navy should be abandoned while she was still afloat. The struggle to make oil connections went on for three days and was finally accomplished.

Back on shore duty in the states, Beach discovered that what had once been called "Rickover's Folly" was now spoken of with the hushed voice of awe. The performance of the *Nautilus* had made her the most admired ship in the Navy. On her shakedown cruise she had traveled 1,381 miles, entirely submerged. She ran faster submerged than on the surface, and had run 62,562 miles before a new load of uranium was put in. Another atomic sub, the *Sea Wolf*, remained submerged for 60 days while cruising 14,500 miles.

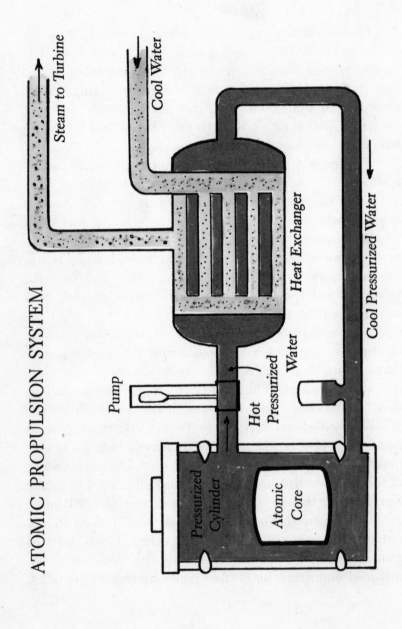

ATOMIC PROPULSION SYSTEM

Steam to Turbine

Cool Water

Heat Exchanger

Pump

Hot Pressurized Water

Cool Pressurized Water

Pressurized Cylinder

Atomic Core

The atomic submarine was making history. The Navy was progressing in the field of nuclear propulsion more rapidly than had been believed possible. Plans were being made to build as many as 100 atomic powered submarines. Oil burning ships were becoming things of the past. A flood tide of change had begun, and Beach would have to learn about atomic energy or be left hopelessly behind the times. Blueprints had been made for the largest submarine in the world. Beach hoped that he might command it.

He wrote later, "I became aware that I might command *Triton* when the time of my prospective sea duty and the launching of the new ship seemed to fit together. I felt that a submarine of this size ought to have a captain as Commanding Officer, since she was to be, in fact, the size of a light cruiser. I applied directly to Admiral Rickover and was informed that he would consider giving me his approval if I was willing to go through the training program."

To see how nuclear fission was transformed into a propulsion system for a submarine Captain Beach took off his uniform, forgot his Navy rank, and went to Idaho Falls to study Rickover's Mark I—the prototype atomic engine of the *Nautilus*. It was to be an intensive three-month study with an intervening period of less strenuous work, but Mark I was scheduled to be closed down for servicing in seven weeks, shortly after the Fourth of July week-end.

Rather than continue the study again in the fall, Captain Beach decided to cram the entire three months study into seven weeks. It meant an eighteen-hour day, seven days a week, working right through both Memorial Day and the Fourth of July. He had to learn how to operate the hundreds of gadgets that comprised the instrumentation system. He had to learn the name, the location, and the function of each of thousands of parts.

Examining the entire system of Mark I in detail, Beach for the first time appreciated what a miracle Rickover and his group has performed. Here was an engine that would not break down in a rough sea as did those of *Trigger* on her shakedown cruise. Before him was the perfect engine that Jules Verne could only describe with fuzzy vagueness.

Beach completed the training about mid-July. On weekends and holidays, when everyone had departed, there was nothing to eat but candy bars from slot machines. He lost fifteen pounds, but he knew now how to run an atomic engine. His final written examination, which lasted 14 hours, he passed with the skill of a professional.

He never lost his sense of awe toward the atomic reactor. Whenever he peered through the heavily leaded glass windows at the mysterious forms which contained the ghostly white atomic fire, he marvelled that nothing went in and yet so much heat came out. The invisible fire never seemed to consume itself. It might have seemed spooky had he not known in detail the all-powerful laws of nature that made it function.

What a contrast to the noisy, greasy, grimy diesel engines! They would operate only with a constant flow of oil. Submarines on war patrol had to travel thousands of miles back to base to replenish fuel supplies even when there were still torpedos left in their tubes. Thirty days of his 60-day patrols were spent going to and from battle areas. The 350 tons of fuel oil could last only so many days.

But the jug-shaped vessels in the center of the *Triton* were an almost inexhaustible source of energy. Like Captain Nemo in Jules Verne's masterpiece, he could roam the sea for years with the *Triton* without worrying about fuel. So mighty was the power of the *Triton* that it had to be fitted with a million dollar instrumentation system just to keep it under control.

Aboard the *Triton*, the nerve center of the propulsion system was in a special room brilliantly lighted with fluorescent tubes. Men stood before dials that kept a continuous record of pressures, temperatures, flow, and levels of coolant and feed water.

In this room man proved himself to be master of the machine. The watchers kept a fingertip control over the movement of the graphite rods that moved in and out of the reactor in the adjacent compartment. The rods increased or decreased power as needed. Other men watched dials indicating the movement of the swift river of water that raced through the tubings. They kept a constant check on the temperature, pressure, and velocity of the water that flowed in and out of the reactor.

The fissioning atoms performed like a well-trained prancing circus horse, kept in rhythm by the slightest flip of a whip. Their silent explosions were kept in a steady tempo, releasing just the amount of heat to keep the steam turbines whirling and turbine generators pouring out the electric power for the population of this undersea town of nearly 200 souls.

Chapter *6*

Eternal Vigilance

The smooth operation of the *Triton* lulled Captain Beach into a feeling of confidence in his ship on the first night of the trip. He was able to sleep soundly, and he rose refreshed the following morning.

When he woke there was no way of knowing, except for the ship's clock over the door of his tiny stateroom, what time of day it was. He groped from his curtained cabin toward the eerie red lights of the control room.

He had left orders to steer the *Triton* clear of the submarine operating areas, and then follow a straight course for St. Peter and St. Paul Rocks, lying far off the bulge of Brazil, 3,250 miles south. The Captain made a beeline for the chart table to see what point on the globe the submarine had reached, and whether it was time to change the ship's clocks. In the Navy, it is the duty of the Officer of the Watch to trace a line on the chart during each watch period. The line indicates where the ship started, the direction it is moving, the speed, and the distance traversed hour by hour.

A water speedometer indicates the speed, a compass the direction, a chronometer the time. This method of keeping tabs on the ship's position is known as "dead reckoning," since it is accomplished without celestial aid. A great deal of the art of the navigator is involved, because the effect of current can only be known through experience and study.

The *Triton* had swung far out to sea before heading south so as to avoid bucking the swift, north-flowing current of the Gulf Stream. Furthermore, the *Triton* was on a secret mission, and it was important that it reach its destination unseen. Captain Beach had plotted a course that avoided the usual shipping lanes.

Captain Beach going over the plot of the ship's course

The charted position of the ship corresponded very closely to that indicated by the Ship's Inertial Navigation System (SINS). The rows of flashing dots in SINS winked cheerfully, revealing the information that was being constantly stored in its mechanical brain. Because this was the first mechanical navigator built especially for a submarine, it would require daily checking to test its accuracy. The officers of the *Triton* would have to make periodic star or sun sightings and compare the results with the position indicated by SINS. The Captain would have to raise the *Triton* to periscope depth—about 60 feet below the surface —in order to make the sightings through the periscope.

During the voyage, coming up to periscope depth was to be a daily procedure lasting about an hour and serving several purposes aside from navigation. It would permit the radio antennae to stick out above the surface and receive news and messages. It would allow the *Triton* to raise its air-induction mast (a snorkel device) to pump in fresh air, thereby conserving its precious supplies of oxygen for use when really needed or in case of emergencies. The slower speed necessary during this period would offer the chance to eject garbage bags, human waste, and wash water.

While the diving officer was making the delicate adjustments to raise the submarine to periscope depth, Captain Beach recalled the far more difficult task faced in the oil-burning subs of his previous commands. In the old subs, as fuel burned out, sea water automatically filled the empty space in the tanks. As tanks emptied of oil and filled with sea water, they became heavier. A 1,000-gallon fuel tank weighed 1,300 pounds more when filled with water than when filled with oil. To compensate for the added weight of water, the diving officer had to pump water from the trim tanks near the fuel tanks; sometimes he also had to add water to trim tanks at the other end of the sub to keep her level.

The atomic power plant of the *Triton* had eliminated this problem altogether. The water flowing through the reactor was in a closed system; so was the feed water heated to steam in the heat exchanger and used to turn the steam turbines. The coolants were used over and over again and none were consumed. Thus the atomic propulsion system produced no change whatever in the weight of the submarine.

As the diving officer gave his commands to decrease the sub's depth, two planesmen handled the bow and stern hydroplanes exactly the same way as the pilot of an airplane handles his controls. The flat surfaces of the hydroplanes, extending out from the hull forward and aft, could steer the ship up or down as needed. Other men operated the trim pump which filled or emptied the trim tanks. This was often necessary when changing depth because changes in water density at different depths would of course require corresponding changes in the ship's internal weights.

At the same time, a crewman at the periscopes operated a control overhead to raise them. Hydraulic oil hissed into the hoisting pistons. Two bright, stainless steel cylinders, eight inches in diameter and four feet apart, rose from the flooring up through the watertight fittings overhead. At the bottom of each cylinder was a rubber eyepiece. Since only a tenth of the horizon could be seen at one glance, each periscope was made so that it could be turned to scan the whole horizon. A pair of handles attached to each periscope enabled the navigator to "walk" the periscope around the complete circle of the horizon.

As the periscopes and other masts rose above the surface, the radarman was now able to switch on his green fluorescent screen. Glowing dots indicated the location of distant ships in the area. When the radio antenna was raised, the radioman was able to tune in to news broadcasts. His typewritten sheet of news was to be the main feature of the *Triton Eagle*, which he was to edit and mimeograph for his 183 readers. The snorkel began sucking in fresh air and thoroughly ventilating the interior. The ship rolled gently in the surface swells, with only a few little sticks visible. The rest of the ship stayed submerged and invisible.

Captain Beach wished he could dispense with the snorkel altogether. He had heard that a really effective oxygen generating system was nearly ready, and that it would be installed in all the Polaris submarines. With the new system, mountain-fresh air would be made available from sea water without the need of sucking in air from above the surface of the sea.

A new device, however, had already been added to the periscope to simplify the method of getting a fix on a celestial body. Captain Beach or the navigator could search out certain fixed stars and snap a button just as they crossed the hairline of the periscope device. The click of a recorder printed the time and measured the angle.

It was really simple compared to the heroic methods he had to use previously. Nuclear subs offered all kinds of advantages, and easy celestial navigation was one of the added improvements.

During pre-nuclear days, submarines had to surface shortly before sunrise or just after sunset to get sun or star sights to fix the ship's position. Only twice a day can one see both stars and the clear horizon. The navigator had to wrap his sextant in a towel to keep off flying spray. He had to brace himself against the conning tower, catch a star between clouds, and at the same time catch a glimpse of the horizon.

With the sextant in his right hand, he adjusted the scale with the fingers of his left. When he had the mirrored reflection of the star near the horizon, he would sing out "Stand by," and when he had the star exactly on the horizon he would shout "Mark." The officers below him in the conning tower would repeat the shouted signals to the man in the control room who wrote down the exact second of time indicated by the chronometer beside him.

The navigator then read off the degrees and minutes of the altitude of the star from his sextant. Calculations from tables gave him a "position" line which he drew on a chart. Repeating the process with other stars, he would have several position lines, all of them passing through the same point—if his calculations were accurate. This point was the position of the ship.

All this painstaking and elaborate work was now eliminated with the new device on the periscope. There was no longer any need to surface and "shoot" from the bridge. Periscope depth was now sufficient. And since the horizon was found from a gyroscope, star sights could be taken at any time stars could be seen. But scientific invention was moving at such a rapid rate that even the need for periscope depth might soon be eliminated.

Would SINS make the periscope device obsolete? It was disconcerting to the skipper to find the figures in SINS corresponding so closely with his own findings obtained through celestial observation. A mechanical brain, at one stroke, was eliminating a human skill that had required a lifetime to perfect. The question still remained, however, whether SINS was durable and foolproof. The answer would be known at the end of the voyage.

SINS, in fact, calculated the ship's position in an altogether different way from celestial navigation. Behind its mysterious green, glowing tubes there was a platform, a "stable table," aligned horizontally with the center of the earth. It was held in this fixed position by a series of gyroscopes revolving at phenomenal speeds. Sensitive electronic devices instantly registered any kind of pressure that would move the platform out of its fixed position.

Any change in acceleration, any change in direction or speed, any pitch, roll, or heave of the submarine were registered on instruments in the same way that a person in a moving car senses pressure on his body when the car speeds up, brakes, or turns. SINS measured pressures resulting from the movement of the ship and the movement of the spinning earth.

Here was an array of gyroscopes and accelerometers that recorded every moment of the ship as it slipped through the water. All kinds of information—the spin of the earth, the speed of ocean currents, the speed and course of the ship itself—kept pouring into the Navigational Data Computer (NAVDAC). Out came position references. These, in turn, fed continually into a bank of 16 electronic brains known as the Geo-ballistic Computer. This uncanny brain would digest the position facts in fractions of a second. It would indicate on its dial the precise, pin-pointed position of the ship in relation to the true north. And the numbers of latitude and longitude changed even as the ship itself moved.

But the mechanism was so intricate there was doubt that it could survive the long circumnavigation.

On that first morning after the *Triton* breathed in sufficient fresh air and exhaled the air made stuffy with 183 breathing humans, the order was given to go deep again. The inboard induction valve, however, would not close. An inspection plate was removed and a rusty old flashlight was found, left in the tube by some careless workman and forgotten.

Twenty years before, the submarine *Squalus* lost half its crew because the inner valve of the air induction would not close. The sub submerged, depending on the outer valve to keep the sub airtight. For some reason, the outer valve snapped open again, and water poured into the huge 36-inch pipe, drowning half the crew before compartment doors could be locked to save the rest.

To avoid the repetition of this kind of tragedy, all submarines now had an automatic panel board that showed whether important valves of the ship's ventilation system were open or shut. If there were any open exit on the ship's hull, the panel board would automatically reveal a circle, indicating that electrical circuits for the diving operation had been cut off. When the exit was closed, the circle changed to a horizontal bar.

Older subs had a pattern of red and green lights for this purpose, and the panel was called a "Christmas Tree." But eye tests during the war had proved that the green lights damaged night vision, whereas red lights did not.

Furthermore, when the control room was lighted only with red lights, green could not be seen at all! Finding that a red indicator is very easy to see when red light is the only one available, designers of the new submarines put red bars and circles on their new panels. The alignment of the bars alone signified that all holes in the hull were covered and secure.

The incident of the rusty flashlight brought concern to the Captain. There can be no mistakes on a submarine. Men who are relaxed are more prone to human error than men who are alert. The comfortable appointments of the *Triton* might in themselves lull the crew into a false sense of security.

Everything had been arranged within the submarine to smooth the shock of entering an alien world. There were no real, rough edges of existence for the crew. The interior of the *Triton* was designed to include all the air-conditioned, upholstered comfort of a luxury hotel, except the feeling of spaciousness.

The Crew's Mess Hall was well lighted, finished in cream with pastel pink and green panels. Formica-top tables seated about 46 men. Each table had pull-out metal benches with foam rubber, leather-covered seats. The mess hall could be readily converted into a theatre, where the latest movies were shown twice daily. The room included a juke box with new recordings, a hi-fi unit, a library and an icebox that could be raided at will.

Eight to ten men shared each of the partitioned sleeping areas with its tiered bunks. Each bunk had its own overhead light, an individual ventilating control, foam rubber mattress, plastic covers that could be zipped up when the bunk was not in use, and a plastic hanger bag in which each man kept his clothes.

The decks were covered with attractive inlaid linoleum. Stairways had wide, safe treads. Accordion-fold doors eliminated the hinged door that could suddenly swing out and cause an accident. Shaving mirrors boasted fluorescent tubes above and below. Eyesoothing pastel shades gave the maximum possible illusion of airiness and space.

There was no need to stint on water as on some older ships. Highly efficient evaporators converted sea water into fresh water. Stainless metal drop sinks and high pressure showers were in ample supply.

Electric precipitators performed a noiseless, efficient job of removing particles of grease, dirt, or smoke from the air. No grimy, greasy, smelly machinery was exposed anywhere. A lady in high heels could walk through the *Triton* from bow to stern and imagine herself walking through the corridors of a luxury liner, with the single exception of the many water-tight doors and high coamings she would encounter.

Each compartment had its loudspeaker. A crewman had only to turn a switch to hear music which played almost all the time on a hi-fi tape reproducer. In the depths of the sea, man challenged the unknown with a song. But music, too, might contribute to making the men too relaxed.

The crew had to be made conscious that they were moving through a constant field of danger. That was the loneliest part of being a skipper—the heavy responsibility for all the young men's lives. Submarining was a young man's service. The average age was about 28. It was up to the

Captain to keep them alert to the fact they were living under conditions in which an emergency threatening even their lives could conceivably occur at any moment.

At any moment the *Triton* might crash into an unknown underwater mountain or be dragged down suddenly by an undersea convulsion of some kind. The diving planes might jam in their diving positions causing the ship to nose down too sharply, unable to pull out of heavily pressured depths. The tough skin of iron that separated the *Triton's* crew from extinction might be pierced at any moment. Torpedo tubes, induction valves, and ejectors penetrated through the hull to the heavy sea, where high pressure water was waiting only for a chance to rush in.

The skipper was not a disciplinarian of the old school, but he knew from long Navy experience the wisdom of repeated drill. Constant drilling was the only way to instill automatic responses. He had insisted upon his men standing watches even before the ship had been commissioned. It was well that he had.

There had been a fire on board while the *Triton* was still being built. A deep-fat fryer in the galley was improperly wired; it overheated and set fire to some cooking oil. The construction workers dashed away from the dense smoke and leaping flames, but the two Navy men on watch plunged in, grabbed an extinguisher and extinguished the fire. Navy routine, however, had trained them to make a thorough investigation. They were not through yet. They found the deck above to be surprisingly warm. Suspecting that the fire had spread, they chopped a hole in the ventilation shaft. Flames leaped up at them from electrical wiring.

[85]

They doused that flame and had the fire completely under control by the time fire trucks arrived.

Captain Beach was happy to place commendations in the service records of the two men. They had prevented serious damage to their ship. Their type of eternal vigilance was the price of safety.

Daily drills were imperative. The Captain decided to devote three hours each afternoon to fire drills, collision drills, radiation drills, combat drills—all kinds of drills over and over again. In case of any emergency the men would know automatically where to go and what to do. Through familiarity they would move at double speed, and without the danger of confusion.

There never could be enough drilling. A delay of seconds by one man with a crucial job might prove injurious, even fatal, to all. With every alarm, each man had to be at his station in double-quick time. Each man stood before his particular switch, knob, or lever, his earphones in place, alert to the voice of command. Officers made reports to the Captain from all parts of the ship. Valves had to be opened or closed, and switches thrown within a time limit set by the Captain. The goal of these drills, like that of practicing the hundred-yard dash, was to do them in less time, and better.

Alarm signals were set off for test every day at 12:45 p.m. because they, too, had to be constantly tried out if they were to work when really needed. And each drill, whether fire, chlorine gas, or whatever, had its own procedures. Men at the trimming tanks awaited the order to flood or empty

[86]

the trimming tanks. Men in charge of the hydroplanes stood ready to push or pull the control "sticks." Men in the motor room kept their eyes on the engine room telegraph operated from the control room. Men stood poised before the vent-and-blow panels ready to blow ballast tanks. Watertight doors between compartments were locked tight. Fire extinguishers had to be removed from bulkheads, ready for instant use. Even the cook had to know which valve to turn in his compartment, which lever to pull, which switch to snap, and in what sequence.

A special alarm warned of imminent collision. Its piercing crescendo was a scream that could awaken the dead. It might warn of an impending collision, or it might signal that one of the compartments was flooding. There must be an instant closing of watertight doors to seal off a specified damaged section in order to prevent flooding of the entire ship. Because of the greatly added weight in the ship, even the sealing off of a flooded compartment might not prevent the ship from sinking to the bottom of the sea. The escape hatches must be put in instant readiness. These escape trunks, fore and aft, would be the only exits from a sinking submarine.

Every submariner had undergone months of training for just such an emergency. A special escape tank 18 feet in diameter and 100 feet high had been built at New London, Connecticut. Students at the submarine school first had to learn in a decompression chamber how to equalize pressure on their ear drums. They had to learn to adjust themselves to pressures of up to 50 pounds per square inch, more than three times the normal air pressure of about 14 pounds per square inch.

They made the water ascent in the escape tank in groups of two or three. They entered a compartment at the bottom of the tank. The compartment was flooded until only the head and shoulders of the men were above water. They breathed this heavily compressed air for a minute or two, then the compartment completely flooded. They went upward through the tank, whistling out the heavily compressed air through their mouths.

They learned about the two great dangers of all sea divers—the "rapture of the depths" and the "bends." Both can be fatal.

The "rapture of the depths" is caused by carbon dioxide accumulating in the lungs because the lungs do not work efficiently under heavy pressure. The carbon dioxide causes the diver to become sleepy. He is drugged, and begins to dream. The feeling is pleasant, but highly dangerous because the brain no longer operates rationally. Visions of all kinds take the place of reality, and the diver might find himself delighted with a mood that could lead to a loss of consciousness and possibly death.

The "bends" is caused by nitrogen bubbles in the blood and in the tissues of the body. There is nitrogen in the air we breathe, and there is always a certain amount of it dissolved in the blood. But under heavy pressures, more and more of the gas becomes dissolved in the blood. If the pressure is released suddenly because the diver rises too fast, the nitrogen bubbles out of the blood and tissues just as bubbles arise when a soda water bottle is opened.

[88]

When the bubbles press on nerves, muscles, and tendons, they can cause painful contractions—the "bends." Bubbles in the inner ear can cause deafness, giddiness, or dizziness. Bubbles in the spinal cord can cause paralysis of the legs. If large bubbles press on the brain, they can kill.

Drills, however necessary for the crew, could become in time dull routine. The Captain and the psychologist aboard the ship knew that good food and pleasant surroundings could never compensate for the tedium of routine duties twelve hours a day in a cramped and confined space. Something else was needed to make that kind of life endurable. What was needed was what Dr. Benjamin Weybrew, the scientific investigator of morale aboard the *Triton* called "Motivation."

It was this, the need for a reason for their trip, which convinced Captain Beach that the time had arrived to let the *Triton* crew know their special assignment. On the afternoon of the day following departure, Captain Beach lifted a microphone in the control room and his voice was carried throughout the ship.

"Now hear this, men—"

The *Triton*, he told them, was to circumnavigate the world on her shakedown cruise. The official starting and return point was to be at St. Peter and St. Paul Rocks, 700 miles off the coast of Brazil. The *Triton* would sweep south around Cape Horn and into the Pacific, then would cross the Pacific by way of Easter Island and Guam to reach the Philippines. She would snake through the Philippine Islands to the Celebes Sea, Makassar Strait, the Flores Sea, and

Lombok Strait into the Indian Ocean. She would take the great circle course around the Cape of Good Hope back to St. Peter and St. Paul Rocks. From there they would move up to the Canary Islands and the coast of Spain and then cross the Atlantic back to home.

They would be entirely submerged all the way. They were on a pioneer voyage of exploration and endurance that would benefit mankind and add a shining page in world history. Because they were duplicating the feat of the first circumnavigator, the underwater voyage would be known as Project Magellan.

The announcement had the impact that the Captain hoped it would have. Later he wrote, "Whenever I paused, I had the feeling that a penny dropped anywhere in the ship would have sounded like a hammer blow on an anvil."

There was no doubt that morale and motivation, at that moment, reached a peak. The hubbub in the mess room could be heard all over the ship. Everyone tingled at the prospect of being a charter member of an historic voyage. There was a brightness in the men's eyes, an alertness in their bearing as they went about their watch duties. The Captain was confident that this new purpose that had entered their lives would overcome all difficulties.

Chapter 7

Busy Bees Underseas

After the first surge of enthusiasm, the crew began to have sober thoughts about the miles and miles to go before they would be back "at liberty" in New London. Drills might fill up part of the time, but there were still many hours left to kill. Crew members began to gravitate towards hobbies, classes, and tournaments that broke out in a rash all over the ship.

Fifty hobby sets were auctioned off and winners were soon absorbed in number painting, clay modeling, mosaic, and leathercraft projects. Card players signed up for tournaments in bridge, pinochle, acey-deucy, and cribbage. There were also checkers and chess tournaments. Those who wanted to improve their personalities signed up for a public-speaking class.

Many of the crew who were ambitious to advance in rank used their leisure hours to attend classes in *Triton's* "College of Undersea Knowledge." This was a sort of "self-help" school. Specially qualified members of the crew gave lectures to the others on mathematics, history, civics, Spanish, and French.

Almost every man aboard had to "walk pipe." With

[91]

instruction manuals in hand, they had to follow the pipes of the water, air, steam, and hydraulic systems all over the ship. The constant possibility of an emergency demanded that each man know as much about the ship as was possible. It soon was a common sight to see pairs of men moving from compartment to compartment. The qualified man had a check list in his hand. The other, studying for qualification, tried to figure out the purpose and function of each valve.

Watching movies was, of course, the most popular recreation. There were eight o'clock and midnight showings in the mess room. When the tables were cleared and the seats rearranged, there was usually a scramble for the best seats, and many men had to see the movies standing. More decorum was observed in the wardroom where officers had their own movie showings. But the new movies were always shown to the crew first.

Members of the crew who preferred reading a book or magazine could do so on the narrow cubicle of their bunks with their small, private, overhead lights. The bunks were the only spot in the overcrowded ship that provided a little privacy, but even this was not always the case, for there were not enough bunks for all the people on board. In a submarine jammed to the brim with machinery, each man had to content himself with 1.5 square yards of space, and about 50 had to "hot bunk"—which meant that three men had two bunks to sleep in. This worked pretty well, since one of the three was always on watch.

Commander James E. Stark and his four Navy hospitalmen were responsible for the physical health of everyone on board. Dr. Stark was both Ship's Medical Officer and Atmosphere Control Analyst. He was an experienced physician with a master's degree in radiation biology.

A neutron-film badge and a small dosimeter which measured X-rays were provided to each man. These devices were worn clipped to the shirt front, and they indicated for each person the nuclear radiation level he had actually received. The ship had a radiation laboratory, fitted out for testing and checking on the flying neutrons from the nuclear reactors. Operating the laboratory was also Dr. Stark's responsibility.

The five men were kept busy around the clock. Each watch had its schedule of radiation checks, which included reading instruments located at different positions throughout the ship, and processing air samples taken from the engine room and the reactor compartment. Every two hours they checked on the oxygen content in the ship's atmosphere, the percentage of carbon dioxide, carbon monoxide, and other gases. The sealed atmosphere of the sub was healthful, almost as good as the air outside. The oxygen content was held at 20.3 percent, carbon dioxide at 1.5 percent, and carbon monoxide from 10 to 20 parts in a million. Oxygen was kept at a uniform level by "bleeding" it into the ship from tanks around the hull. Machines called burners and scrubbers held the other gases at very low levels.

The nuclear reactors were, of course, the points of greatest interest. The reactor-shield instruments were kept under observation at all times. Liquid samples from various portions of the engineering plant were examined every four hours. Once a week all compartments had to be sampled for surface contamination. Badges on each man were collected once a month and inspected for indications of darkening, which revealed whether radiation had gone beyond the permissible level, (none ever did). The pocket dosimeter, a pencil-like instrument, could give a reading of the total amount of radiation accumulated by holding it up to a light. Thus each man could quickly check on himself anytime he wanted to.

There was a 400-ton air-conditioner unit which freshened and recirculated the air throughout the ship every two minutes. Although electrostatic precipitators constantly filtered air for smoke, grease, and odors, Dr. Stark had his assistants go around the ship with foot-long vacuum cleaners to collect samples of the air. The tiny particles collected were screened and accumulated for later testing to find out what precisely floated about in a sealed atmosphere. Dr. Stark was trying to determine just what caused the characteristic submarine smell which permeated clothing. There were also some mysterious chemicals that led to eye-smarting from time to time.

The Doctor took extra precautions in stocking up with medical supplies. *Triton's* pharmacy was also his responsibility, and he wanted to be ready for whatever might come.

The sick bay, or infirmary, was set apart from the radiation laboratory. At the beginning of the voyage, everyone caught everybody else's cold. It required about thirty days for the men to reach complete immunity from colds.

The other "health" man, Dr. Benjamin Weybrew, was head of the Personnel Department of the U. S. Naval Medical Research Laboratory at the Submarine Base in New London, Connecticut. His investigation of morale was considered vital to the Polaris submarine program.

Weybrew was interested in the psychological effects of long periods of submergence on submarine crewmen. He wanted to learn the effects of too much carbon dioxide, the ability to tolerate aggravating situations, mood fluctuations, sleeping habits, and performance efficiency. Weybrew lived in the crew's quarters so he would have full opportunity to observe them.

It was a difficult assignment. He had only five days notice before sailing date, just time enough to get his necessary equipment together and suggest that the ship acquire the fifty hobby kits that were later auctioned off to the crew. It was no easy task, either, for a Doctor of Philosophy to rub shoulders exclusively with men much younger than he, and whose studies were all in the mechanical rather than the sociological field. His very mission in itself would almost certainly create underlying resentments. The *Triton Eagle* tried to help with an article stating that he was no bona fide "head shrinker," but it wasn't long before he heard himself jokingly called a spy who had a direct pipe line to the highest ranking "head shrinker" in the Pentagon. The crew, however, gradually came to realize that his investigation could be the most important aspect of the circumnavigation, and that his analyses and suggestions might very well determine future Navy policy toward long-confined crews in nuclear submarines.

The U. S. Navy was frankly worried about enlisting submariners for the Polaris program. Dozens of submarines were in the blueprint and building stages. They would have to be manned by two crews each, with more than 100 men and officers in each group. The crews would take turns making the long patrols, the off-duty crew catching up on shore leave and receiving training ashore. Thousands of men would be needed. Dr. Weybrew was supposed to find out what was required to keep the submariners who had to undergo these strenuous schedules happy enough to want to reenlist.

Weybrew's previous reports on nuclear submariners had been disturbing. The stresses of prolonged undersea life were more than most men were willing to accept without some special return for their special sacrifices. Everything possible had been done on the *Triton* to reduce these stresses. The Navy was eager to see the final report card that Weybrew would present at the end of the voyage.

The morale investigator handed out mimeographed sheets to the fifty men who volunteered to keep track of themselves in a daily mental health survey. They were to check off on a list those states of mind which best described how they felt. This gave the psychologist a good cross-section of the daily record of sleeping habits, tensions, interests, drives, aches, pains, and enthusiasms. These daily fluctuations of moods of the fifty men would be represented on a graph which, it was hoped, would indicate what needs of a submarine crew were satisfied, what preferences or dislikes they experienced, and what combination of factors released the most productive energy in them.

There were men aboard from the Hydrographic Office in Washington. They were equipped with a new Precision

Depth Recorder instrument which took soundings about 30 times a minute and recorded them on a moving roll of paper.

This machine measured the distance to the bottom of the ocean by calculating the time required for a sound signal, moving 4800 feet a second, to travel from ship to ocean floor and back. A pen drew a profile on the moving paper of the ocean bottom under the course of the ship. This machine was of special importance to the *Triton*, because of the constant danger of bumping into the tops of unknown sea mountains.

On the second day out, the Hydrographers released their first orange-colored bottle, a procedure they were to follow once or twice a day. The sealed bottle fitted into the signal injector and floated out on its own buoyancy to the surface. Inside the bottle was a sheet of paper, printed in several languages, with the following request to the finder:

"If the finder of this paper will return it to the U. S. Navy Hydrographic Office, Washington 25, D. C., direct or through any U. S. Consul, he will thereby assist in the verification of the circulation of ocean currents. His services will be very much appreciated by all mariners."

He was asked to list his name and address and to fill the blank spaces which noted the time and place where the bottle was found. There were, of course, spaces where the name of the ship putting the bottle into the sea was supposed to be written, but this could not be done for fear that some of the bottles might be found before the trip was over. Instead the initials "MT," standing for Magellan-*Triton*, and a serial number were used.

Years later when enough of these bottles from hundreds

of ships are washed ashore they will indicate the meandering paths of the currents sweeping through the 140 million square miles of ocean.

Early on the morning of February 23, the depth recorder signaled an unknown mountain that rose 9,000 feet above the ocean floor. Actually, the mid-Atlantic contains a portion of the greatest mountain range on the earth—a mountain chain that meanders 40,000 miles through all the oceans except the northern part of the Pacific.

One section of this chain, the Atlantic Ridge, rises near Iceland in the middle of the Atlantic Ocean and runs as far as 50 degrees south, midway beneath the continents of South America and Africa. This ridge is 500 miles wide and 10,000 miles long with many peaks rising from 5,000 and 10,000 feet above the sea floor. The highest peak of the Ridge is Pico Island of the Azores, rising 7,000 feet into the sky out of water 20,000 feet deep.

The sharpest peaks of this same ridge are the cluster of islets known as St. Peter and St. Paul Rocks, the immediate destination of the *Triton*. The highest rock is not more than 60 feet above the sea. Its summit is constantly sprayed by the mist created by the waves beating against the islets. Some legends claim these barren islets are the remains of Atlantis, the mythical continent that was supposed to have sunk into the Atlantic in prehistoric times; but of this there is no proof of any kind.

The galley was the busiest place on the ship. Its electric stoves were in constant use cooking the 600 meals a day for the three crew sections. The steward had stored 82,585 pounds of food for 75,000 meals. There were 3 tons of flour, 2 tons of sugar, 1,820 pounds of coffee, 20,000 pounds of meat, 460 pounds of cake mix, 935 pounds of ice cream mix, and many other foodstuffs.

The foods brought into the *Triton* were dehydrated, all fat and bones removed, and squeezed under tremendous pressure to take up the least possible space. When the crew loaded the ship for the journey, wherever a bit of space on the *Triton* was found empty, it was immediately filled with the cans, cartons, packages, sacks, and boxes that overflowed the regular storage space.

The cook was delighted with his stainless steel paradise, which had all the latest improvements in automatic cooking. The cold storage, deep freeze, and ice cream compartments operated at top efficiency. The Captain and some of the older hands recalled the World War II days, when an ice cream machine had to be improvised and the ice cream, more likely than not, had the flavor of diesel oil.

Among the modern equipment in the galley was the garbage disposal unit. Trash was gathered into nylon-mesh bags and dropped into a heavy bronze tube which reached all the way down to a door in the bottom of the ship. It worked exactly like a torpedo tube. The top had to be tightly fastened before the bottom door could be opened and then the nylon bags, weighted with bricks would drop to the bottom of the sea to avoid any tell-tale grease or oil stains on the surface of the ocean.

A few days after departure, the outer door of the garbage disposal suddenly jammed and brought an unex-

[99]

pected crisis. In all the other subs Captain Beach had served in, the garbage was put into sacks and dumped overboard once a day or so, whenever the sub surfaced to recharge its batteries. But the disposal unit in the corner of the galley, an essential addition to the most modern of submarines, now turned out to be a grim hazard. Not only could it not be worked; the outer door had jammed open. Only the weaker inner door held the insistent ocean at bay!

For a while, garbage had to be ejected through a torpedo tube, but only at the expense of fouling up the torpedo-ejection mechanism with refuse. After nightmarish hours of exploration, the cause of the jamming of the outer door of the disposal unit was discovered to be simply over-greasing of the mechanism. Some of the grease was removed and the unit functioned again, but the Captain brooded over the narrow escape from catastrophe. It brought home the fact that any little thing, like over-greasing, could bring an under-sea ship near to disaster.

The enlisted men were kept so busy keeping their iron monster moving safely beneath the sea that there was little time to nurture a grievance, pine for a sweetheart, or become lumpish with boredom. The Captain himself was kept hopping as a new crisis presented itself almost every day of the shakedown voyage. Even as the *Triton* raced toward the official starting point of the circumnavigation— "the Rocks"—a new anxiety loomed up. The Rocks were so tiny, they might not be sighted by periscope, if they were just a few miles away.

For 36 hours an overcast sky had made all celestial

navigation impossible. SINS had begun to act strangely and could not be completely relied upon. The Navigator had to depend on the compass, speedometer, chronometer, and his best estimate of current, actual distance traveled, and ac-

St. Peter and St. Paul Rocks seen through a Triton periscope

curacy of steering for a dead-reckoning calculation of the position of the Rocks. The *Triton* rose about noon on February 23 to periscope depth. There was no sight of anything above the surface of the sea. Minutes went by without success, and the first twinges of gloom deepened on the *Triton*.

To locate his position on the empty wastes of the ocean by means of a pinpoint of light in the sky is one of the sensuous delights of a sailor. But to locate your position without such help, and to see land suddenly appear where you said it was going to appear, is an even greater thrill. At 12:03, the periscope sighted a tiny white dot on the horizon. The Executive Officer, who was also the ship's Navigator shouted in jubilation. All the officers congratulated him on a good job at the most difficult form of navigation—dead reckoning.

The few-hundred-feet-long jagged peaks were completely bare except for an abandoned lighthouse and a skyful of birds. But J. Baylor Roberts, the National Geographic photographer, who was also a Commander in the U. S. Naval Reserve, was delighted with the challenge of snapping his first photographs through a periscope.

Chapter *8*

Captain and Crew

Captain Beach brought a heart-warming informality to the *Triton*. He conducted himself as a shipmate as well as a skipper, creating a tone of comradeship so important in the early stages of a voyage. He believed there was no need to make a display of rank with a severe look, a measured step, or an imperative tone of voice.

The way Captain Beach saw it, he had not weakened discipline.

"The distinction [between officers and men] hasn't been blurred. Just the manner of its observation. A little informality on the part of myself or one of the other officers goes a long way. The objective is an attitude of willingly working together in which the little expressions such as 'yes, sir' are unconscious habit and therefore inconspicuous. The formal structure of discipline, while always meticulously observed, becomes the *servant of efficiency* and remains in the background unless, infrequently, it has to be invoked."

The crew began to recognize they had an unusual skipper—a man with instinctive, but relaxed authority. His friendliness made it easier for them to live in crowded conditions under an authoritative system that demanded constant drills and regimentation.

And yet morale began to sag when the novelty of the long voyage began to wear off. Sluggishness set in, due possibly to the lack of exercise and the semidarkness of the sleeping quarters. There was very little privacy in the bunk room with someone always climbing up or down or walking past the berths. A walk through the passageways from bow to stern meant pushing past ten or fifteen others, each one muttering "pardon" or "excuse please."

The psychologist began to notice that some men seemed to wake with slight headaches and a sense of not having slept well. They were saying, "I feel like sleeping all the time." There was a drowsy look about them as if they were hibernating animals dozing away the winter. Other men made "The Prisoner's Song" a popular number on the hi-fi, playing it over and over again as if the poignant music spoke out for them. There were times when Dr. Weybrew wondered if there might be too much carbon dioxide in the atmosphere.

A confusion of time set in. Men would wake up and wonder whether it was day or night. It really didn't matter because there was no sense of motion, and they might still be back in Block Island for all they knew. The confused time perception, however, brought embarrassing moments. One man rose at 8:30 a.m. and began to get ready for Bingo scheduled for twelve hours later. Another man arose at 1:30 in the morning and thought it was afternoon. They would greet Dr. Weybrew with a good morning in the afternoon and a good night in the morning. The men whose watches were set from 4 a.m. to 8 a.m. and from

4 p.m. to 8 p.m. were the most likely to be confused.

During the first two weeks, the crewmen found release in chattering about their wife and kids. They would whip out a photo at any display of interest. But the homesickness, sluggishness, and confusion began to disappear after two weeks. There were fewer headaches and less difficulty in sleeping. Family life began to recede to the distant past and the remembered future as life on board became more absorbing.

The weekly cycle began to be measured by Fridays, when all the crew readied for officers' inspection. At 8:50 in the morning, the loudspeaker system blasted out, "Up all bunks, rig ship for white!" Because of the long hours of watch, it was the only day all hands were waked in the morning. If the voice on the loudspeaker did not wake them, the sounds of the alarms, five minutes later, certainly did. "Test of all alarms. Disregard alarms." Then came the weird, unearthly sound of the radiation casualty alarm, to be followed by the "eeooga" of the diving alarm, the shriek of the collision siren, the musical bong-bong of the general alarm. "Test of alarms completed. Regard all alarms!"

The different groups all over the ship had to work hard to pass inspection, which began after lunch and was not completed until 5:25 p.m. Compartments had to be immaculate, and each man had to memorize his check-off list for any quizzing by the officers. To most of the men, inspection time seemed a day of extra work, and they grumbled about it. But it did keep them alert, and it was a break in monotony.

The day following inspection, was Saturday, no drills. But the regular duties of running the ship went on as always.

For relaxation there was taped music going all day long—everything from Beethoven to Montevani, from rock n' roll to hillbilly to jazz. Next day was Sunday, a day of rest, of writing letters, of reading—and standing watch.

Both Catholic and Protestant services were held on Sundays. Enlisted men and officers volunteered to deliver the sermons at the Protestant service. Captain Beach preferred to call the "sermons" moral lessons or talks, since only an ordained minister can deliver a sermon. The capacity of 46 seats in the mess room was never filled, somewhat to his disappointment, but there was a loyal core of devout men who found great comfort in the singing and responsive readings from the Bible. Captain Beach was brought up in a Christian household and he believed very strongly in the power of faith. Lieutenant Pat MacDonald, Reactor Control Officer, went out of his way to urge everyone to see the movie, "Out of the Deep," produced by the Moody Bible Institute of Chicago. There were at least a dozen men on the ship who read the Bible daily and with reverence.

For Captain Beach, the voyage had only begun as the *Triton* bored through the sea towards the Falkland Islands off the southern coast of Argentina. This was the second leg of the long voyage. Would he reach them without a mishap? His long sea experience had taught the skipper to expect the unexpected aboard a ship—and it came on the morning of March 1.

The Precision Depth Recorder—also called a "fathometer"—was reported out of commission. This was a serious blow, since it would be crucially needed in the shallow waters approaching Cape Horn. It was also the most precise means of warning against unknown sea mountains. Now the Echo Ranging Sonar would have to serve as a substitute.

The sonarman had to be more alert than ever. As he turned his control wheel, he listened intently to the pitch of the eerie, hollow sounds. A change in pitch could tell him whether the ship was closing on or moving away from any obstruction.

Sonar equipment sends out a steady series of pings. Sound travels four times faster in water than in air and can be heard ten times as far away. After hours of endless pinging, there may come an echoing pong. Is it a ship, a school of fish, or the bottom of the sea? A sonarman requires lots of experience to differentiate the different types of returning echoes, or to tell sound of the screws of a ship from the similar rhythmic throbs of a school of porpoise.

Sonar had other limitations. Sudden changes in temperature in the water can cut the sonar's range from miles to a few yards. The Captain could only pray that sonar would give sufficient warning if ever the *Triton* happened to be on a collision course with a mountain top or an iceberg. But being a practical seaman, he also doubled the sonar watches and put the ship's best men on them.

More disturbing news arrived when Doctor Stark reported a very sick shipmate aboard. The chief radarman was in excruciating pain, probably from a kidney stone. There was no special X-ray aboard to diagnose the patient, nor the special medical equipment to operate. The radar-man had been given a sedative, and the doctor could only hope he might be able to pass the kidney stone.

Later that night the electronics man reported that the fathometer was working again. As a result of constant use, two crystals had overheated, expanded, and cracked. Of the 60,000 items in the ships' repair parts inventory, there were none for the fathometer. On surface ships, fathometers are usually used only when the ship is in shallow water. But the *Triton* had been using hers continuously, and it had com-menced to overheat. There had been no previous experience of a fathometer breaking down, and consequently the Navy had made no provision for replacement parts. The electron-ics repair department finally improvised a new circuit, but the men said they could not guarantee against another possible rise in temperature.

The following day, the chief radarman seemed to have made a dramatic recovery from his illness. He was back at work, taking apart one of the radar units that needed repair.

Meanwhile, the *Triton* was approaching the Falkland Islands and it was necessary for the Captain to be sure he was moving toward his target. Again there was a chance the islands might be just over the horizon and might be missed. Once again overcast skies ruined the chance of get-ting a fix on sun or star. As in the case of the approach to the "Rocks," the skipper had to rely on dead reckoning, which indicated the Falklands should be only 35 miles away.

A mood of anxiety prevailed on the ship. There was danger in the air. Icebergs were to be expected in that far

[108]

south latitude and there was a general uneasiness over whether the sonarman would be able to detect them in time to prevent a collision. The recent trouble with the fathometer had been a warning. It might recur. And Chief Radarman Poole had had another attack, after several hours of freedom from pain. Some of the crew began to worry that the *Triton* would never make it around the world. Something, somewhere was bound to crack.

The *Triton* rose to periscope depth to try to make a radar contact with the islands. After 15 minutes of groping with the radar, a pinpoint of light glowed on the radar screen. Another perfect landfall! The photographer was ready to snap pictures of the Falkland Islands through the periscope, from a distance of five miles away so that the sub could avoid detection.

The *Triton* was near the Antarctic Circle, and the sea was very rough. Though submerged, the ship was rolling as much as 10 degrees when Dr. Stark appeared before the Captain, his face unusually solemn. The radarman had had a serious relapse. Not even a morphine injection could relieve his excruciating pain.

The Captain hurried down to the lower deck to see for himself. One of the hospitalmen, assigned the nursing watch duty, was standing on a ladder to be near the sick man, who was lying in a top bunk. Poor Poole, too drugged to make a coherent statement, was moaning and writhing in agony.

The Captain was faced with one of the lonely moments of command. The nearest place he could transfer the patient off the sub would be at Montevideo, Uruguay, 1,000 miles north. Would the *Triton's* mission be ruined? To enter port he would have to surface and make himself known to the authorities. Who could have foreseen that a submerged and undetected round-the-world voyage would collapse because of something as tiny as a kidney stone?

Ever since the first signs of Poole's illness Captain Beach had been debating the problem. It need not be an either-or-decision. There was a third possibility; the U. S. Navy itself might be able to come to the rescue. Fortunately, a radio report had been received that the *USS Macon* was headed toward Montevideo harbor. He could arrange a midnight rendezvous with the cruiser, and make the transfer. There would be no need to surface, and the secrecy of Project Magellan would be saved. The *Macon* had facilities for taking care of the sick man.

Everything now depended on the availability and cooperation of the cruiser, but there was no time to lose. Captain Beach phoned the Officer of the Deck and ordered him to reverse course back to Montevideo harbor and to increase speed to maximum.

One hour later the *Triton* slackened speed and was raised to periscope depth to transmit a message to the Navy Department. The skipper of the *Macon*, was Captain Reubon T. Whitaker, a good friend of Captain Beach and a renowned submarine skipper during World War II. This bit of information Captain Beach gleaned from a Navy manual in his office. He also learned that the *Macon* was the flagship of the Commander, U. S. Forces, Southern Atlantic under the charge of Rear Admiral E. C. Stephan, who had been Beach's squadron commander back in 1949. If it were

[110]

at all possible for them to do so, these two friends would come to his help.

Short-wave reception was poor during daylight hours. It required more than an hour for the *Triton's* short wave radio to make a contact, which happened to be on the island of Guam on the other side of the earth. Guam, with its powerful station, promised to forward a message requesting the *Macon* to meet the *Triton* 2 a.m. on March 4th at a specified point off Montevideo. The spirits of the *Triton's* crew soared.

The *Triton* went back down into the sea and resumed her race north, moving at a speed so phenomenal that if the periscope masts or the antennae were to be raised they would have been snapped off or bent. Strangely enough, the higher the speed the steadier the *Triton* became, as if she were specially built for excess momentum.

Toward midnight the ship was slowed down for periscope depth to catch any radio messages that might be addressed to the *Triton*. The Navy came through with the best possible news. The *Macon* would be able to meet the *Triton* at the time and place specified. The good news went through the loudspeaker all over the ship.

The Captain was now faced with one of the most difficult technical operations demanded in the control of a submarine. The transfer of a man from a sub to a whaleboat on a heaving sea would require a virtuoso performance by a master submariner. The undersea ship had the length of two city blocks, and to lift it out of the water by inches would be a supreme test of captain and crew working as a unit with split-second efficiency. It was like having a giant seabeast perform a miracle of balance, moving ever so slowly in a medium that was rising and falling with changeable swells.

The "sail" of the *Triton* containing its conning tower, bridge and masts was like a four-story elliptical building, 25 feet high above the deck of the ship. With the upper part of the sail out of water, the hull could still remain submerged while the conning tower hatch could be opened for egress of Poole and his transfer to the whaleboat of the *Macon*. In this way the *Triton* would be obeying the letter as well as the spirit of her mission.

As long as there is no change in the size or weight of a properly trimmed submarine, she will be in balance. She will neither rise nor sink. Of course her size does not change, but the buoyancy of the water in which she swims may. And as food is consumed and waste disposed off, the sub becomes lighter. If the weight is lost at the stern, the stern will rise. The distance of the lost weight from the center of gravity determines how much tipping force will be exerted. To get the sub back to level, the diving officer has to know how much water to add (in this case) to the after trimming tank.

A diving officer must keep a very careful record indicating weight and position in the ship of all supplies taken aboard. He has charts showing how much weight must be added to which trim tanks to make up for losses in weight.

The diving officer must also take into account the temperature of the sea water. Warm water expands, occupies more space. It is lighter per cubic foot than cold water.

Hence a submarine which is in perfect trim in cold water will start to sink in warmer water. The more salt in the ocean water the heavier it is per cubic foot; so saltier water makes the sub start to rise.

Normally, a diving officer knows the feel of his ship so well that he can recognize instantly if the ship is off trim. His judgment is so accurate that he can detect differences of only a few hundred pounds in a submarine weighing millions of pounds.

Even more difficult than reaching neutral buoyancy is the ability to maintain it. Owing to the movement of men about the sub and the changes in the density of the surrounding water, it is sometimes impossible to maintain this precarious balance. The surface of the ocean is always moving, heaving, swelling—turbulent enough to turn the stomach of all but the sea-hardened. The Captain realized that because of all these factors he was heading toward a major test for himself and his ship.

All through the following day while the *Triton* was hurrying back to Montevideo, the speed indicator above the throttlemen's station was at a point that her crew found hard to believe. Even more startling were the readings of the various gauges in the maneuvering room. With all her amazing speed, the *Triton* was not even beginning to use her real potential. In a time of battle crisis, with all stops pulled, the *Triton* would be able to go even faster. Most gratifying of all was the fact that the faster she moved the steadier she became. There seemed a curious relationship between size and speed of the nuclear ships that was prom-

[113]

ising for the gigantic ships of the future.

Submarines are free from the retarding action of the pressure waves which hold back surface vessels. Since there was no such wave to retard her speed, Triton's top submerged speed, for example, required half the power needed by comparatively sized surface ships to attain such a speed. The larger the ship, the more efficient she can be because carrying capacity increases at a more rapid rate than the power needed to drive the hull through the water.

At 2 a.m. on March 5, the Captain ordered periscope depth. As the double periscopes slid upward, the Captain bent down, snapped open the two handles of one of them and put an eye to the eyepiece while the periscope was still rising. In its fully raised position, it allowed him to stand comfortably at his full height, with his arms crooked over the handles. He turned the periscope rapidly through a complete circle, his body moving around with it. Finally, he came to rest on one bearing. He saw the Macon against the night horizon waiting for him. Both sub and cruiser had arrived at the precise point and time agreed upon.

Now came the crucial test—to keep the 8,000-ton ship 99 percent under water. It was like playing an organ that consisted of 86 miles of piping which circulated compressed air at a pressure of 400 pounds to a square inch. Enough air pressure was admitted to the main-ballast tanks to keep the conning tower just five feet out of water. The skipper climbed to the upper conning tower compartment and ordered the lower conning tower hatch shut. Then the upper conning tower hatch was ordered open a quarter of an inch. Water squirted through the crack and the hatch was shut quickly. The sea swells were still splashing over the bridge above the conning tower.

The *Triton* had to be raised a little higher. Through a speaking tube, the Captain ordered a short blast of high pressure air into the most forward tank, which raised the bow about a foot. When the hatch was again raised a quarter inch, no water swept in. A two-minute wait for the action of the swells proved that the bridge was now above the peak of the surface waves. The hatch was flipped open and the Captain jumped out. The hatch was then quickly closed to within a quarter-inch margin; a quartermaster was stationed at the hatch to close it completely if water started to come in. The *Triton* had "broached" the surface.

Topside, there was fair visibility despite a drizzle of rain. The *Macon*, 500 yards away now, was letting down a motor whaleboat. The bridge-command speaker on the *Triton*, despite the weeks of submergence, was in perfect working order, and the Captain was able to communicate with the men below in the control room. The radarman was told to report the range of the *Macon* from minute to minute so as to keep track of any possible dangerous drift of the two ships towards each other.

The skipper then called the handling party topside with all the necessary gear. Each man was to have an inflatable life jacket with attached flashlight and a safety belt hooked around him with its traveler. Submarine Force regulations require every man going topside on a submarine to wear a strong canvas belt with a chain and strong sliding clip attached.

[*115*]

This safeguard came as a result of several tragic accidents. Men on the topside of a submarine had been swept overboard and drowned by sudden huge sea waves. For this reason all submarines now have a topside safety rail. The sliding clip is clamped over the rail and slides smoothly along this safety track. When two men have to pass each other, they simply exchange chains with each other, unsnapping and resnapping them to their belts.

As the whaleboat of the *Macon* approached, the Captain studied the deck of the submarine from his perch on top of the conning tower. *Triton's* forward deck was about a foot above the water, the aft submerged.

The Captain observed that an occasional sea inundated the area around the conning tower. This might be dangerous for Poole in his weakened state. It would be necessary to raise the forward section another foot.

"Control, this is the Bridge, blow forward for one second." Air whistled into the tanks forward for a long second. The area of the conning tower rose another foot or two. Permission was granted to have the handling party go down on deck. They affixed their clips to the track. A mooring cleat was rotated upward to fasten the whaleboat's bow. As the whaleboat neared the sub, a sudden high swell rolled over the foredeck, soaking the men up to their necks. Fortunately, the travelers held them secure.

The whaleboat came alongside. Its line, thrown to the handling party, was fastened around the cleat. Two men in the boat held her off from the side of the sub with reversed boat hooks.

Radarman Poole, bundled up and supported by Dr.

[116]

In the dead of night, the sick man was taken off the submarine.

Stark and Lieutenant Sawyer, squeezed through the hatch-door to the deck. They watched for the moment when the gunwale of the boat came level with the edge of the submarine deck. When the chance came they pushed Poole quickly into the boat where waiting arms caught him and led him to his seat. He had not even got his feet wet.

The line was quickly cast off, the boat hooks pushed hard, the whaleboat's engine was gunned, and seconds later it was speeding back to its mother ship. A few minutes later, the expected radio message arrived. "Bridge, this is Radio—from the *Macon*—Poole safely on board." The entire operation was completed in less than an hour.

After the *Triton* submerged again, there was a deep feeling of thankfulness for the way the Navy had come through. A new surge of confidence swelled over the crew. Each of them now had proof that in back of every man in the Navy stood the strength of a world-wide organization with 700,000 men, 900 warships, 10,000 aircraft and 300 naval bases.

Chapter *9*

Cross Currents

To make up for the time lost on the mercy mission, Captain Beach ordered the *Triton* to head at maximum speed toward Cape Horn.

The *Triton* reached Cape Horn, "Old Cape Stiff," as seamen have called it, on March 7. The crews of surface ships were often "frozen stiff" while making the crossing, but the *Triton* maintained its comfortable 72 degrees temperature. Her rocking motion, however, left no doubt that at Cape Horn all the currents of the world meet in turbulence.

At the shallow depth of 60 feet, the *Triton* rolled rather heavily. And yet she was a cozy haven as she traveled through the 12-foot waves, the 25-knot winds, and the rain squalls of the surface. Sailors on windjammers would have had to battle all day amidst freezing spray and howling wind to cross this small passage of water.

Each of the crew members was given "periscope liberty" to see the Cape. After three weeks underseas, the sight of gray, cold-looking water, swirling spume-driven whitecaps and Old Cape Stiff himself was a revelation of another world. The color-hungry eyes of the submariners feasted on the enchanting sight.

When the *Triton* reached the calm waters of the Pacific, the skipper decided on an especially difficult drill. Both reactors were shut down and the diving crew was ordered to maintain depth and course on manual control and to keep the submarine in perfect trim.

It is not too hard to keep a submarine level while it is going full speed. The very momentum carries it along on a level plane. Without power, however, the huge *Triton* was like an elephant trying to stand on one foot for a long time. It did it clumsily, but one marveled that it could be done at all.

The *Triton* would move up or down depending on the temperature and salinity of the ocean depth. Lieutenant Hay had the complicated job of calculating the changing weights and movements aboard ship so as to shift the exact amount of water from one trim tank to another until the bubble of the inclinometer was in the exact center.

In time of war, a motionless submarine is very difficult to detect. If it finds an underwater current, it might be able to drift away from any enemy surface vessel probing for it.

Eventually, the characteristics of ocean depths at any spot of its 140,000,000 square miles will be known to submarine captains. Collecting this information is the vast program that the Hydrographic Office in Washington has set for itself. A submarine skipper would then be able to choose the best thermocline (layer of water of different temperature) on which to hover and escape.

After the diving drill, the "nuki-pooh" boys, as the men working on the reactors were called, had only to make an adjustment of the control rods to get the reactors back in operation. After that, maintenance again became comparatively easy. Unlike the greasy "snipes" of the old diesel subs, the "nuki-pooh" boys sat before their clean, streamlined consoles, keeping an eye on pointers and gauges with an almost bored expression.

Five days after rounding Cape Horn, the *Triton* made radar contact with Easter Island. Once again periscope liberty was granted. The entire crew stood in line to get a glimpse of a famous orange and crimson statue that is the most mysterious feature of the island. Nothing now remains of an ancient civilization of Easter Island, whose warriors plied the oars of long war canoes back and forth between the isles of the Pacific. Nothing survived but the strange angular statues they left behind. The meaning of the statues could only be guessed at.

Near the most prominent statue was a pink stucco house, a nicely graded dirt road and a well tended garden that might be part of any prosperous suburban community.

Two days later on Sunday, March 13, the sub was at its closest point of approach to Pearl Harbor, Hawaii. A ship's party had been planned for that occasion, and the crew was resplendent in aloha shirts and beachcomber outfits. The cooks prepared the sumptuous dishes of a fancy Hawaiian luau. The high point was reached when hairy-legged "hula dancers" swung to the rhythm of a guitar and a set of bongo drums.

The Captain had allowed the crew to take complete charge of festivities. He felt it was important to let them

[121]

improvise a diversion on their own. They built a palm tree and designed the huge cake, two feet square. The Executive Officer, Commander Will M. Adams, could not resist the chance to prepare the Hawaiian paste, "poi," that is made from the taro root and is eaten with the fingers. Poi, Adams insisted, was indispensable for a Polynesian luau. He was able to provide that authentic note with a know how acquired in his younger days at Pearl Harbor.

The *Triton* crossed the International Date line on a Wednesday which automatically changed the day to Thursday. One day had vanished. But the day lost in the westward movement around the globe had to be made up by a series of 25-hour days. Every fifteen degrees of surface covered from east to west lost one hour of time on the *Triton's* clocks. The numerous clocks on the ship were in a constant state of jitters. No matter how accurately they ticked they were always racing ahead of the zone time and had to be turned back about every third day. For the men on watch, their four-hour stretch often turned out to be a rubber band.

The hydrographers were gathering a lot of information, but they complained of the limitations of the *Triton*. They frequently wished that the *Triton* were as advanced as Jules Verne's wonder ship, to which he had given powers of vast illumination to the depths and an access hatch onto the sea floor. Sometimes, as they prepared bottles of water from different Strata of the sea, they were conscious of the swish of water at the bottom of the submarine. If they could only "see" as well as "hear" the ocean depths!

They knew that day was not far away. A "maser" de-

[122]

vice can now shoot a beam of light for a distance of a mile with the spread of only an inch. The waves of light march out in step instead of piling out of the tube helter-skelter, as they do from an ordinary light source. This light can perhaps be amplified and made to illuminate the dark depths of the ocean.

The hydrographers were only one step away from the glass lookout of Jules Verne's *Nautilus* that sent its electron beam as a ray of light opening up the vistas of the bottom of the ocean to the eyes of man. What fantastic sights might some day be revealed? Some of the great gashes on the bottom of the Pacific Ocean are as huge as seven Grand Canyons and as long as the distance from New York to Kansas.

Along the equator, the *Triton* bucked the most gigantic river in the world—the Cromwell Current. With a thousand times greater flow than the Mississippi, the Cromwell current is 200 miles wide, and flows eastward at 100 to 1,000 feet below the surface of the sea. It flows for a distance of 7,000 miles at 2.5 knots. It lies beneath two slow westward currents on the surface, one of which carried the famous raft Kon Tiki from Peru into the islands of the South Pacific.

The men from the Hydrographic Office—Nick Mabry, Gordon Wilkes and Mike Smalet—busied themselves with checking their instruments. They took gravity meter readings, pitch and roll records, water temperatures, and salinity measurements at different depths. The data they collected would become part of the millions of pieces of information sent in by submarines and would one day help to make the depths of the sea as well known as the surface of the earth. The three men, in fact, were doing for the depths what the "father of hydrography," Matthew Fontaine Maury, had done for surface currents 100 years ago.

Captain Beach had a personal reason to be interested in hydrographic studies because of a tragedy in his father's life. His father had been the skipper of the cruiser *Memphis*, when it was lying peacefully at anchor in Santo Domingo harbor in the West Indies. Suddenly, without any warning, a tidal wave came in from the sea, drove the ship on the rocks and utterly destroyed her.

Some 70 men of the *Memphis* lost their lives in the catastrophe, a number of them in a boat which was bringing a baseball party back to the ship. On board, a number were killed by flying debris and burst steam lines. The skipper's life was saved by his Marine orderly, who shoved him inside just before the bridge went under. When the ship came back up, half the people who had been on deck were gone, including the skipper's orderly.

Now the son, skipper of a submarine incomparably more powerful than the old *Memphis*, was carrying on an expedition designed to, among other things, eradicate the possibility of such a thing ever again happening without warning. Captain Beach rightfully resented the Navy habit of calling the *Triton* a "boat." The 8,000-ton submarine had more horsepower than a World War II battleship, and deserved to be called a "ship."

The skipper gloried in her power as she raced across the Pacific. Textbooks might mention only some bare facts about her—keel laid, May 29, 1956; launched, August 19,

1958; sea trials, September 25, 1959; commissioned November 10, 1959; departed February 16, 1960 to circumnavigate the world. But in between these dates, he had listened to hundreds of lectures, plowed through heavy tomes on physics and thermodynamics, mathematics, and electrical theory just to get a nodding acquaintance with his amazing "boat." Thousands of men in laboratories, steel mills, electronic plants, warehouses, and factories all over the country had labored for this Navy "boat." She had cost the United States $109,000,000. For Captain Beach, the *Triton* was a ship, the symbol of America at her technological greatest.

Chapter *10*

Ordeal of Battle

The Pacific held a flood of memories for Captain Beach. They were turned loose by a radio dispatch announcing that Roy S. Benson had become the new Commander of the Submarine Force of the Navy's Pacific Fleet. Benson had been Beach's navigation and seamanship instructor at Annapolis and later his skipper aboard the *Trigger*. Now that Beach was moving through familiar sea lanes, he could remember his World War II years on the *Trigger* as if it were yesterday.

No hunter can forget his first kill. Beach's had happened just 20 miles off the coast of the southernmost Japanese home island. The large shadow on the horizon that he saw on his midnight watch turned out to be a cloud of smoke. It came from an enemy vessel moving without an escort.

The *Trigger* kept seven miles from the target so as to be out of sight. It raced its four diesel engines to full power in order to get in front of the freighter. Because the *Trigger* had only four knots more speed than the Japanese ship, it took hours to get into position.

Remaining fully surfaced, the *Trigger* ghosted in to about 1,500 yards from the approaching ship. It was up to the skipper to get everything set for the torpedo salvo. The torpedos had to be aimed at so many yards ahead of the moving target. The skipper had young Beach train the bridge "Target Bearing Transmitter" to the exact middle of the target so as to keep track of the constantly changing picture, telling the attack party exactly what was happening on the surface.

The distance, direction, and speed of the target and the direction and speed of the sub were fed into an electronic device. This device figured where a 45-knot torpedo should be aimed so that it would meet a 15-knot ship which would have moved 500 yards during the time that the torpedo was traveling. The answer was expressed in degrees, the direction at which the torpedo should travel in order to hit the target at the end of the run. Before the torpedo was fired, it was set so that the rapidly turning gyro wheel would guide it in the proper direction. But with the target a mere blob in the dark night, it was easy to lose it or misjudge the angle. Everything depended on the skipper's judgment. When he cried out "Stand by to fire!" and then shouted "Fire!" he was risking his years of training and reputation.

Two torpedos were fired within a ten-second interval. After a long, tense wait of more than 60 seconds, the boom of an explosion came loud and clear, followed within a few seconds by a second explosion. Almost a year of study and practice by an entire crew paid off in two bull's eyes. The tension in the submarine exploded into loud, exultant cheers.

The *Trigger* circled and watched her first victim go under—a necessary observation in order to get official credit for a sinking. Loud rumblings and crushing noises could be heard through the sonar gear. The squeals and groans of tortured steel were like something alive, struggling against death. But at the last moment, the anguished ship recovered its dignity, accepted the inevitable and quietly slid beneath the sea.

The *Trigger* remained submerged the following day, patrolling the area near the southern entrance of the Inland Sea. No ships were sighted. She surfaced again that night to recharge her batteries. Suddenly a lookout saw a destroyer heading full speed directly toward him.

All the officers of the *Trigger* had practiced crash dives until they were sick of them. But this one was for real.

"Dive! Dive!"

The diving alarm let out two "eeoogas." The destroyer would be upon them in about 120 seconds. Within that time, the *Trigger* would have to dive down deeply enough to escape the full blast of the first depth charge.

What each man did had to be in harmony with what dozens of other men were doing at the same time. A submariner is like a player in an orchestra, keeping one eye on the score before him and ears cocked to the voice of command. Each man's life now depended on getting down at the maximum rate of 60 feet a minute, down to below the safety zone of 100 feet.

The lookouts and officers on the bridge tumbled down the small round hole of the hatch in a prearranged sequence within 11 seconds. The last man banged the hatch after him and locked it with a hand wheel.

The engineer pulled a lever which switched power from diesel to batteries just in time to prevent the diesels from consuming in seconds all the life-giving air in the sub. Other men in the engine room raced around to shut the valves which had been opened while the diesel had been pumping exhaust overboard.

The Diving Officer sang out a rapid string of commands. A rush of air escaped through the vents of the ballast tanks, allowing water to flood in and pull the *Trigger* beneath the surface. Two men had already stationed themselves before the two huge wheels controlling the bow and stern planes, and put the sub into full dive. The rudder was centered amidships.

The helmsmen reached up to turn off the electric fans and the air-conditioning system so that no turning motor would be heard by the sonar gear of the enemy.

Standing before the panel of red and green lights, the Diving Officer signaled for the closing of the main air-induction valve. It closed hydraulically with a sharp thump. The "Christmas tree" turned all green, indicating that every vital opening in the hull was closed. By this time, the sub was sliding down at a sharp 20-degree angle. Water sloshed over the conning-tower. Only 20 seconds had elapsed since the alarm.

"All ahead, two thirds."

The planesmen manipulated wheels to control the angle and depth of the dive. The forward fins tilted upward to lift the bow.

"Flood forward trim from sea."

The bow was coming up a little too fast, and the flooding of the forward trim tanks slowed it down slightly.

"Secure flooding!"

The rumble of water rushing into the trim tanks stopped. The men at the diving planes wrestled with the big wheels to keep the boat at the desired angle.

At 35 feet down, the *Trigger* seemed to pause, wasting precious seconds. The order was shouted to flood more tanks to get the sub diving faster. The sonarman switched on the amplifier, and the horrible drumming noise of the approaching destroyer could be heard throughout the ship.

Now came the most critical maneuvering. The Diving Officer had to be careful not to put the sub into a nose dive. If too much water were admitted, the sub would sink at an increasing rate. If it could not be stopped, the sub would reach depths where the hull would collapse from the tremendous pressure.

The sub was driven at two thirds speed to get away from the destroyer and to keep from going into too steep a dive. Then speed was decreased to one-third so that the propeller noise would be less likely to be picked up by the destroyer's sonar gear.

By this time, the *Trigger* had sunk about 100 feet and was ready for depth charges. Since all the fans had been shut off, the temperature within the hull began to rise rapidly. All the watertight doors were shut. The approaching destroyer's roar almost froze the brain with the horror of an imminent explosion.

The sonarman heard the splash of the first depth charge dropping into the water above him. It rushed down at ten feet a second, preset to explode at a certain depth. The one grave danger, now, was that the preset depth would be exactly the same as the submarine's depth. If it would explode within about 30 feet of the sub, its hammering shock wave might burst a hole in the submarine's hull, flooding a compartment. This would mean a bull's eye for the destroyer. One flooded compartment alone would send the sub to the very bottom.

The explosion hit the *Trigger* with the impact of a giant sledgehammer. Beach was almost knocked off his feet. All the pipes and fittings vibrated. The light bulbs swung crazily on their two inches of exposed and insulated wire. Locker doors burst open. The air was filled with flying bits of dust. Steel bulkheads squeezed inward and sprang out again.

"Check and report all compartments!" the skipper's voice came through the loudspeakers. Reports came back from eight watertight compartments. There was no water leak anywhere. The *Trigger* had held up under the near miss. The depth bomb barrage, however, had only begun. The *Trigger* continued to move down to its lowest possible safe depth.

The screws of the destroyer slowed. The Japanese were waiting for the underwater disturbance caused by the explosion to calm down so they would be able to relocate the sub.

The *Trigger* kept twisting and turning to present the smallest possible target to the enemy's probing sound waves. When the intervals between successive pings became shorter, the sound man on the *Trigger* knew that the destroyer had found the sub and was coming in for another run.

At the next explosion, the hull rang like a tuning fork. The sub whipped convulsively. The men who gripped the large stainless-steel wheels felt the shock to the marrow of their bones. The electrician's mates gripped the crucial levers and switches, knowing their very lives depended upon keeping them in place. But the *Trigger* proved itself to be solidly built. Only a direct hit would shatter the hull.

The depth charges and evasive tactics went on for hours. The temperature in the sub reached 130-degrees F. Everyone had stripped down to his undershorts. The planesmen and helmsmen exuded so much sweat and energy to hand-control the giant fins and rudder that they had to be relieved every five minutes. Breathing became difficult as the carbon-dioxide content mounted. Carbon-dioxide absorbent was spread over the deck. Salt tablets were passed around to compensate for the heavy sweating.

During the nerve-wracking pounding, young Beach tried to control the surges of fear that came hot and cold with sickening effect. His ears were cocked to the noises made by the screws of the destroyer. The pinging sounds went on endlessly, sometimes toward the sub and sometimes away from it, as the sub twisted continuously.

As long as the pinging sounds could be heard, Beach, like the others, felt helpless and hunted. Men went about their duties with parted lips and staring eyes, and a continual sweating of the palms. Fear reached an acute stage when the screws of the enemy ship suddenly grew louder—as if they were just outside the hull. There was nothing anyone could do but sit it out. No matter how he tried to think of other matters, young Beach found his mind turning back to the swish, swish, swish of the destroyer's propellers, always followed by shattering explosions.

The time came, at last, when the explosions seemed to draw away from the sub and then still further away. An undersea current was causing the sub to drift away from the destroyer. *Trigger's* motors began slowly turning the propeller to get the sub even further away from the now distant explosions. Soon all contact was lost and speed was increased. An hour later, the *Trigger* surfaced and raced away in the fresh, cool sweetness of the pure night air.

Then came the immense relief that was kin to exultation. They had faced the nemesis of death without flinching. None of them had broken down. There were no cowards aboard. It was their baptism of battle and they had survived the worst ordeal of war.

Chapter *11*

Band of Brothers

Searching back into his war memories, Beach was grateful for the privilege of having been a submariner during those days when most men were merely cogs in the war machine. Submariners were a class apart, a small enough group to be vitally interested in each other.

In the stress of battle, the lowest ranking crew member was sometimes as important as the captain. By the end of a patrol each man aboard had reason to thank every other for his very life. Those who endured the agony of depth charges never forgot the upsurge of loyalty and respect for each other —so exalted and so different from anything they had ever experienced before. In those poignant moments the sweating crew, super-efficient because of the stress they all shared, truly became a band of brothers.

The first attack and the first depth charge were part of a pattern that continued all through the war. Almost always, after firing a spread of torpedos the sub had to go down into the depths to take punishment from the inevitable destroyer.

There would be weeks of monotonous searching and then, suddenly, the crash of action. The "eeooga" of the dive alarm . . . Dive . . . Battle Stations . . . Shut the induction

. . . Bleed air in the boat . . . Ten degrees down bubble . . . Easy on the bow planes . . . Blow negative . . . All ahead one third . . . Fifty-five feet . . . Up periscope . . . Bearing . . . Range . . . Angle on the bow, mark . . . Get set . . . Fire!

As Diving Officer, Beach had to learn to be extremely precise. A matter of inches was important. Losing depth control might cause the submarine to expose too much periscope or blind the periscope by sinking it under the water. Expecially after firing torpedos, the sudden loss of weight caused the bow to become light, and approach the surface of the water. This could be fatal when a destroyer was nearby. Sometimes the sub dived too steeply. Then there would be a struggle to tip the bow up and keep the sub from plunging to dangerous depths.

It took time for the *Trigger* to develop into a fighting submarine with a personality of its own. The crew had to learn to get torpedos away within 30 seconds. Always in attacks, the sub had to stalk its prey, lay a trap for him, and then wait for him to fall into it. Each new encounter posed special problems. New angles had to be solved as the target zigzagged in the night. The enemy's next zig had to be anticipated. Many times convoys were followed for days before the right moment presented itself.

The *Trigger*, under Lieutenant Commanders Roy Benson and Robert E. Dornin, became one of the Navy's star performers. On June 10, 1943, the *Trigger* sighted the giant aircraft carrier *Hiyo*, the pride of the Japanese Navy, as she was leaving Tokyo harbor. Four torpedos were fired. Only one exploded. But the ship was crippled and had to be

Combat Information Center—the nerve center of the
submarine

towed back to port. Later complications caused her to sink on
a sand bar in Tokyo Bay. The destroyers accompanying *Hiyo*
gave the *Trigger* a terrible beating, forcing her to go down to
300 feet. How the *Trigger* survived that depth charging is
still a mystery. Beach liked to think *Trigger* had a soul and
the will to live.

A submarine torpedo was a miniature version of the
boat itself. The entire interior was jammed with machinery,

[137]

mechanical brains, and explosives. It had air compressed to 3,000 pounds per square inch, 2,500 different mechanical parts, a gyro that spun at 16,000 revolutions per minute. It could travel 45 miles per hour for a distance of three miles. Its 668 pounds of explosive could tear a 40-foot hole in three-quarter-inch steel. But during a critical period of the war, fully half of the torpedos either failed to explode or exploded prematurely.

A torpedo was fired by first putting it into a tube which pierced the hull of the sub. The inner door of the tube was closed, and the outer door opened. A blast of compressed air forced the torpedo from the tube. The compressed air which powered the torpedo's engine left a tell-tale white wake of air bubbles. These bubbles would give an enemy ship an unmistakable warning. The long minute or two that the torpedo had to travel sometimes gave the enemy ship time enough for evasive action.

But even more disturbing was the fact that many torpedos were mechanically faulty. The explosive cap of a torpedo was a few inches away from the hammer, and many times the two failed to connect. In the early days of the war, five American subs crept through enemy mine fields into Lingayen Gulf where 80 Japanese transports were sitting like ducks. Only one torpedo exploded.

Since each torpedo cost $10,000 or more, they were rarely used in target practice. That a torpedo might have mechanical faults was not believed possible until angry reports came flooding into Navy headquarters from the war zones.

After new devices were worked out to explode the torpedos, there was a dramatic change in the record of sinkings by U.S. submarines. Enemy shipping losses as a whole climbed from 13 ships per month in late 1942 to 48 per month at the peak in 1944. The torpedo turned out to be the most deadly enemy of the Japanese Empire. *Trigger* and her sisters sank ships all over the Pacific.

The failure of the early torpedos eventually proved to be a blessing in disguise. Engineers developed a torpedo equipped with mechanical ears. These were capable of picking up the sound from the screws of the target vessel and zeroing in on the source of the noise.

The success of the *Trigger* brought promotions to Beach from Diving Officer to Engineering Officer and then to Executive Officer. During that time, *Trigger* had four skippers.

Lieutenant Commander F. J. Harlfinger took command for the *Trigger's* ninth patrol, and in an area not far from the Marianas Islands, her radar picked up two escorts patrolling about 15,000 yards ahead of a convoy. *Trigger* was about 12 miles away. In maneuvering to attack it was necessary to dive under the escorts, gambling that the Japanese would not detect her. As it happened, Japanese radar had already spotted the sub, and the entire convoy was alerted.

When *Trigger* came to periscope depth for the kill, she found herself surrounded by destroyers with one dashing in to ram her. *Trigger* had time enough only to fire four torpedos and then she crash-dived.

There wasn't any chance of escape. Six destroyers formed a ring around her, and kept the ring no matter which way *Trigger* moved. Depth charges rumbled insistent warnings that *Trigger* was doomed and that it should surface and surrender. During half the night and into the late afternoon of the following day, the harassment continued.

Her heavy steel sides buckled in and out with each explosion. Cork insulation broke off in great chunks. Sheet metal seams popped loose. Instruments were shattered. Electrical circuits were thrown out of order. The water in the bilges reached a danger point. Water had to be bailed out from the motor compartments to the aft torpedo room by bucket brigade. The temperature rose to 135 degrees and men began collapsing from the heat.

The lack of oxygen made every breath a gasp. Tortured valves began to leak steadily from the constant pounding of the depth charges. Linoleum decks were covered with a film of sweat, oil and moisture condensed from the air. The men at the hydroplanes struggled desperately to prevent *Trigger* from sinking any deeper. The destroyers kept waiting for *Trigger* to run out of oxygen and battery power so that she would be forced to surface. The fleshless and boneless fingers of the Japanese sonar kept their grip on the hull of the sub.

Harlfinger and Beach had just about decided they would have to surface and fight it out to the bitter end, when the sound man reported that *Trigger* was drifting nearer the southern edge of the circle. It was a sure sign that the Japanese were unwary. The rudder was hand-pushed so as to head *Trigger* toward the biggest gap in the circle. The destroyers above seemed to be moving indifferently. Incredibly, *Trigger* found herself outside the circle. As silently as possible she slunk away at one-third speed, then two-thirds speed, and then at last, when no sound of destroyers could be heard, *Trigger* surfaced to race away on her diesel engines

[*140*]

just as another night fell.

Badly damaged though she was, *Trigger* was nevertheless able, three weeks later, to sink four freighters and one destroyer out of a convoy of five freighters and five destroyers. Back in Pearl Harbor, *Trigger* was found to require six weeks for repair instead of the usual two, and was sent to California for the repair job. But on her next trip west, she fluttered 36 miniature Japanese flags and a Presidential unit citation. Also she boasted a blue flag with a white number on it—for *Trigger*, in the opinion of her crew, had become the number one submarine of the fleet.

Beach did not go on the last trip of *Trigger*. He was the last officer of the original crew to leave her. He was ordered to return to the United States for a leave of absence and then to become the Prospective Executive Officer of a new submarine, *Tirante*, which was being built at Portsmouth, New Hampshire.

Beach's leave of absence in June of 1944 was a turning point in his life. His father had died the preceding winter, leaving a great emptiness in his life. He had bared his soul to his father in his letters all through the Naval Academy and the war years. Beach has written of his father:

"I have always revered him. He was 52 years old when I was born—the first of three children by his second wife, the first Mrs. Beach having died a few years before with no children. He retired from the Navy when I was four years old, and lived the rest of his years in Palo Alto, California, where I grew up. While there, he was first a professor at Stanford and later City Clerk and Assessor of the city. I had read all his books by the time I was ten and have always carried a complete set with me."

A wonderful new love filled the gap left by his father's death. He fell in love with the daughter of a Stanford professor. Energetic, capable, and beautiful, she was to prove the ideal life partner for a naval officer. Sea-shore rotation is the lot of all Navy men, but Ingrid said she would rather have half of Ned Beach than the whole of anyone else. Fortunately, she was used to travel. During her youth she went on frequent exploratory trips which her father made for an oil company. Years later, Beach was to write:

"My wife seems to become more stimulating and beautiful all the time. Yet it is also true that the frequent separations heighten the joys of the home, undoubtedly sharpen my intellectual, emotional, and physical hunger for my family. One thing, I think, is definitely true; there are fewer divorces, infidelities, and unhappy homes among Navy men than in any other group."

The honeymoon to Portsmouth, New Hampshire, where the *Tirante* was commissioned, was over only too quickly. *Tirante* set sail for Pearl Harbor in January, 1945. With 31-year old Lieutenant Commander George Street in command, and 26-year old Ned Beach as Executive Officer, the *Tirante* finally entered Japanese waters in March, 1945.

While patrolling the East China Sea, the *Tirante* received orders to meet the *Trigger* for coordinated duty. Beach was eager to see his old home again—so eager, in fact, that a tiny rubber boat was made ready for paddling over to the *Trigger* even before radio contact was established.

The *Tirante* surfaced at the time and place agreed

[142]

upon. But there was no sight of Beach's old sub in the wide expanse of water dancing under bright moonlight. Beach sat near the radioman as message after message was transmitted. No contact was made.

Beach never forgot the nightmarish silence of the following three nights. He hovered over the radio operator who patiently pounded away on his key on the frequency reserved for submarines. The crew spoke in whispers. Cups of coffee were brought in to keep Beach and the radioman awake as the message was repeated over and over again. The radioman, Ed Secard, had also served on the *Trigger*, and the two friends kept their vigil together. There never was an answer. When a submarine is gone, there is only the silence of the bottom of the sea.

It was a staggering blow to Beach, perhaps his most complete realization that war was a game that was played for keeps. He imagined himself living through the horror of those last moments on his beloved *Trigger*. The depth charges must have continued for a long time as *Trigger* twisted and turned 300 feet under. He had heard that the Japanese had a new type of depth charge that could be preset for greater depths than earlier ones. Somebody must have been talking. How else could the Japanese have known?

There it was—the bull's eye that exploded within 20 feet of the control room. The collision alarm screamed for the last time. The hole was too big to hold back the water even with a full blast of compressed air. There would be indescribable confusion as *Trigger* nose dived and everything loose tumbled down against the bulkheads. The depth gauges would spin crazily until they reached their limits and jammed against the stops. Before she hit bottom, the pressure of the lower depths flattened the steel shell of the compartments like a collapsed tin can. The pounding pulses of the men stopped for all time as water under fantastic pressure took possession of their bodies.

Medical scientists report that at the last moments, one not only reviews one's life but also becomes singularly detached from all pain. The pain remains for the loved ones left behind, the friends and associates with whom one has lived and worked, the comrades-in-arms in common cause.

His new submarine, the *Tirante*, was superior to any other sub yet built. It had a stronger hull, more powerful engines, better radar, more torpedos including a "homing" torpedo, and a speed twice as fast as any merchant ship. A dark, implacable mood possessed him as *Tirante* sank a Japanese fishing boat. Such boats were known to radio information on the position of every sub they sighted. One might have been *Trigger's* nemesis.

By the spring of 1945, so many convoys had been wiped out between sunset and sunrise by American submarines that the Japanese merchant ships were forced to hole up in harbors for the night. The *Tirante* was off the harbor of Quelpart Island, about 100 miles off the coast of Korea, when periscope observation noted unusual activity. There were a number of airplanes overhead and frigates on sentry duty at the entrance of the harbor. The radarman noted five shore-based radar stations. Commander Street and Beach agreed there was something important inside the harbor. But charts indicated that the harbor had only nine fathoms of water (54 feet), too shallow for a dive. The *Tirante* would have to shoot it out on the surface.

With the crew at surface battle stations, the Captain running the approach from the conning tower and the Executive Officer aiming the torpedos from the bridge, *Tirante* approached the anchorage from the south to within 1,200 yards of the coast. The Japanese patrol boats showed no sign of recognizing the presence of the sub. They thought, no doubt, that no enemy sub would dare move about through mined waters so openly.

Beach, through binoculars, was the first to spot the ships at the other end of the harbor. The first torpedo, swept by current to the right, just missed a large target and exploded on shore. The next torpedo, corrected for drift, was a bull's eye. The target exploded in a mountainous and blinding glare of white flame, 2,000 feet high, lighting up the entire harbor. It had contained either gasoline or ammunition.

Warships went after the *Tirante* like bloodhounds. Beach aimed the next torpedos down their throats, knocking them out before they could reach her. Then the *Tirante* raced back to the safety of the sea at flank speed.

The exploit won a Presidential Unit Citation for the *Tirante*, a Medal of Honor for the skipper, and a Navy Cross for Beach. But Beach's greatest satisfaction was to have revenged himself for the death of *Trigger* by seeking out the enemy through mine fields and into the very lair of their harbor.

Back in Pearl Harbor, Beach learned that he would be rewarded with a command of his own. At the age of 27, Beach became the skipper of USS *Piper*.

The *Piper* took a long time to get started, delayed by

alterations and new equipment to guide it through extensive mine fields. It was destined to penetrate into the only safe area still remaining to the enemy—the sea of Japan.

Skipper Beach was so eager to get into action, he sailed on the surface all the way to Japan. He maneuvered through several chains of closely laid mines, at one time escaping contact by inches, and finally entered the Sea of Japan. At that moment news was flashed that the war was over. Beach strode the deck alone that night for hours. He could not join in the wild exultation of the crew. A deep despondency settled down upon him. He went to his stateroom, closed the curtain, turned off the electric light and sat brooding in the darkness.

Faces haunted him, the faces of shipmates who would never return home. Why should it have been Penrod, Johnny, Stinky, Willy, and not Ned Beach? Why they and not himself?

After six years of an ever-intensifying life and death struggle, he could not find, now, a new, inward center of gravity. The August night was serene. The stars were bright and beautiful, but they could not bring peace to his soul. Very few had survived the ordeal of so many battles. The final cruel score of submariners killed was 375 officers and 3,131 enlisted men. Their voices from the bottom of the sea demanded an answer.

He had no answer except, perhaps, the promise that he would never forget them. Seventeen years later, the nuclear submarine *Triton* had reached the area in the Pacific where the original *Triton* had been sunk. Captain Beach remembered his promise. It was only fitting that he pay some tribute to the ill-fated men of the old *Triton*, and in this way salute all the lost submariners of World War II.

The old *Triton* had been the first submarine to sink a Japanese ship in the battle of Wake Island. Beach also recalled an acquaintance of his, John Eichmann, who was lost with the *Triton*. The old *Triton's* commissioning plaque, mounted just outside his cabin in the new and fabulous name-sake ship, carried his name where he could not fail to see it several times a day.

The Plan for the Day of Sunday, March 27, 1960 notified the crew that a memorial service would be held at 3:30 p.m. All hands not on watch were to assemble in the Crew's Mess, the Air Control Center, or the Officers' Wardroom.

While Beach prepared his talk to the young men of his ship, he recalled the day, 18 years back, when he was a young man himself. He was among a group of young officers in Pearl Harbor listening to a speech by an old admiral just before they were to depart on their first war patrols.

He would never forget the sincerity in the admiral's voice when he said that he wished from the bottom of his heart that he could join them in this greatest of all adventures. The admiral had devoted a lifetime to building up the submarine fleet, but the privilege of action in the moment of destiny for which he had prepared was not to be his. That distinction was to go to men who were young enough to be his children. Some of them would never come back. Was it worth the price?

At this point the Admiral's eyes glinted brightly, and there was a suspicion of a choke in his voice. It was worth

[*147*]

risking your life for something bigger than yourself, he said. It was the least you could do for a nation that had stood for the freedom and dignity of the individual and was now fighting for its very existence. This war, if lost, might be Armageddon. Years of life were less important than the value of accomplishment—and this was bigger than anything else ever could be.

Beach and the other young officers sprang to their feet and cheered the old man. Something deep had spontaneously welled up in them.

In the memorial service, Captain Beach hoped to convey something of that spirit to the young men of the *Triton* who might have to respond to their country's need some day. The Officer of the Deck was directed to change course to the south, facing the ocean grave of the first *Triton*. All engines were stopped. All men were ordered to attention and directed to face forward.

Beach had probably been a witness to the death of the old *Triton*, though he did not know it at that time. On March 15, 1943, the *Trigger* had attacked a convoy in the same area in which—it was learned later—the *Triton* was also operating. The *Trigger* had been heavily depth charged but managed to escape. Afterward, the men on the *Trigger* heard distant depth charges for almost an entire hour. After the war Beach learned the meaning of these distant explosions. The log of a Japanese destroyer described the hour and position of a submarine it sank. It was the same time and position of the depth charges heard by the *Trigger*. Beach knew then that he had heard the death blows of the old *Triton*. Now, on board the new *Triton* a bugler sounded attention. Everyone joined in a solemn singing of the Navy hymn. Captain Beach read from Psalm 107:

They that go down to the sea in ships . . . These see the work of the Lord . . . their soul is melted because of troubles. Then they cry unto the Lord in their troubles and He bringeth them out of their distresses . . .

Following the scripture reading, the Captain read a prayer that could serve as a committal service for the dead.

"Unto Almighty God we commend the soul of our brothers departed and we commit their ashes to the deep . . . in sure and certain hope of the Resurrection unto eternal life through our Lord Jesus Christ, at whose coming in glorious majesty to judge the world, the sea shall give up her dead."

The Captain then spoke in grave tones of the men whose sacrifice sanctified service in the Navy.

To end the memorial service, the forward torpedo tubes fired three water slugs—the most appropriate salute of one submarine to another. The thuds reverberated throughout the ship. When the war-like sounds died away, the distant sound of taps consecrated the memory of the dead in the hearts of the living. Captain Beach knew that his own feelings were echoed by every man aboard.

Chapter *12*

Guam to Philippines

T he day after the memorial service, March 28, the *Triton's*
periscopes picked up Guam. It happened that one of the
crew, Edward C. Carbullido, had been born on that island
in the village of Agat. He had enlisted in the Navy in 1946,
and almost all his pay since then had been sent back home
to help pay for a new house and for college tuition for his
younger brothers and sisters. He had not seen his family in
14 years. There never was enough money left over for such
a long trip. Eddie was reconciled to wait another six years
when he would be retired and would be able to enjoy the
home that his Navy service had made possible.

Captain Beach was impressed by the young sailor's de-
votion to his father, who had been a Chief Quartermaster in
the Navy and was now retired. Fourteen years is a long time
to be away from home and the skipper's heart was touched.
He appealed to the crew through the *Triton Eagle* to give up
their periscope liberty in order to give the time to Carbullido
to look for his home on the hill at Agat Bay.

After circling the island and photographing points of
interest, the Captain became disturbed by the activity of
planes and helicopters on the airfield. One sharp eye sight-

[151]

ing the periscope could set off a military alert for an unknown submarine. As Eddie searched for his home, the skipper interrupted frequently for a quick appraisal of any possible danger. He decided, however, that people ashore rarely look at the monotonous expanse of the sea and would not likely notice a periscope five miles away and two inches above the water.

The population explosion had hit Guam as well as every other spot on the globe. Eddie was bewildered by the many houses, roads, and cars that filled a hillside he had known only as a wilderness. At last, he felt he had recognized his father's house from photographs he had received from home. One long glimpse, a heartfelt thank you to the skipper, and Eddie had to scramble down the ladder back to his duties for another six years.

Captain Beach revealed a rare sensitivity when he arranged, later, to have an airline fly Eddie back to Guam for two months leave. The Captain paid for Eddie's trip by the sweat of his pen. He was rather disconcerted when Eddie reported on his return that he spent the entire time helping his father manage a filling station.

On the night that the *Triton* left the vicinity of Guam, while the ship was ventilating, the Captain was startled to see the flashing red and green lights of an airplane closing in on him. *Triton* crash-dived immediately. There was worry in the skipper's mind that the *Triton* might have exposed her periscope too long at Agat Bay. Guam headquarters might at that very moment be on a search for an "unknown" submarine. It was a humiliating thought to a skipper who was a perfectionist in every little thing. The perfect record of secrecy might now be ruined because of his indulgence of a sentimental whim a few hours earlier.

The following night, ventilating again, the same red and green lights closed in from the same direction. How had the Navy been able to keep track of him?

"Let's check the star charts," the Chief Quartermaster suggested. A moment later he called back from the chart room:

"Arcturus bears 070° at this time of night, the same altitude as the aircraft sighted." At once the Captain understood. Arcturus was the "red star"—it was known to sailors by its strange coloring. The vividness of the red and green lights was an illusion—the result of refraction because of dampening of the periscope lens. It was a foolish moment for the skipper, but he did not entirely blame himself. The world-wide cruise had to be a top military secret. Discretion was the better part of valor.

Dr. Weybrew, the "morale" investigator from the Navy Medical Research Laboratory, continued his study of the ability of men to endure long confinement. How much boredom and monotony could men endure before reaching a point where they might make a fatal mistake? The round-the-world confinement on the *Triton* was a rare opportunity for such a study. The findings might be helpful later to space navigators.

Previous tests in other submarines had shown that the lonely man at solitary duties, for example, the radar observer at his scope, developed symptoms that progressed in three stages. First came a normal form of irritability, that

[153]

was followed after a time by sleeplessness, known to submariners as "big eye." If "big eye" were prolonged long enough, it could lead to almost complete withdrawal from reality, classified as "long eye." In this last stage, just prior to the breaking point, the confined man would appear to stare right at you but never see you. He would sit and look into space and not talk.

Dr. Weybrew found nothing so extreme on the *Triton*. Almost all the men were well adjusted to their work and proud of being submariners. One man had given up a high-paying job as a factory manager and had found a sense of peace in the submarine service. Another man had had a tragic automobile accident in which his future bride was killed. Submarining was giving a sense of purpose to his shattered life. A third man, who had switched from studying for the priesthood to engineering work on the *Triton* now had time to reflect on his decision. He decided that the soul of man, not that of machinery was his genuine interest, and that he would go back to his previous studies.

A few found creative outlets in poetry. Ten long poems were written on board the *Triton*. Men developed interest in painting and sculpting. One man became an inventor, and worked out a new electronic design for an air-conditioner. Many men found delight in such hobbies as hammering rings out of coins, or making charm bracelets, mosaics, and fancy leathercraft as gifts for the girls back home.

Life was not too easy for the crew. A hundred days is a long time to be away from home. A hundred days away from home and cut off from the world, too, loomed even larger. Day in, day out, there were four-hour watch periods

Crew's Mess Hall was always a hub of activity.

before gauges, dials, and instruments and only such recreation as could be had on the ship.

    Crew's Mess was a focal point for relaxation. Everything
went on in Crew's Mess—movies, bingo, parties, but above

all, eating. The men "cycled" through their ice creams, pastries and pies, steaks, pizzas, and popcorn, as if it were the one great event of the day. As long as delicious food kept pouring from the galley, as delicious food did, no amount of warning about their girth and not being able to get through hatches curbed their ravenous and almost compulsive eating. If necessary, they said, they would slide through the small round exit hatches in greased dungarees.

But as time went on the psychologist noted that many began preferring sleeping to eating. To lengthen their sleeping time, many began eating only two meals a day. Dr. Weybrew already suspected that the most important thing to a submariner was not good eating nor extra pay but a sense of feeling significant. In a world of rates and ranks, status became an all-consuming drive. To raise the re-enlistment rate in submarines, some new status-seeking motive would have to be found. He noticed how eager most men were to win their dolphins, the insignia of a qualified submariner. To win his dolphins, a man had to study all the pipes and valves throughout the ship.

As the weeks lengthened into months it became more and more difficult for the men to concentrate. A general lethargy began to set in. Was there too much carbon dioxide in the atmosphere? Ball point pens did not seem to work too well. Cigarette lighters were hard to light. Matches didn't stay lighted. Everyone became slower in his actions, more careless—too careless, in fact. The skipper had to order men to adhere to the ship's relaxed "at sea" uniform regulations. They were not permitted to discard their socks and skivvy shirts.

The men got rid of a lot of their tension and hostility on bad movies. They hooted loudly at what they called "stinko" movies. In contrast, an exceptionally good movie was like a tonic. They loved Disney's "White Wilderness," good mysteries, scantily clad girls in musicals, and the bright colors of color films. They were deeply stirred by "From the Deep," a Moody Bible Institute revivalist film.

No one failed to look at the map of the world pinned up in a passageway, where Captain Beach and the Executive Officer, who was also the Navigator, indicated the distance covered each day. In an age of jet propulsion, the comparative snail's pace of the *Triton* seemed intolerable. Why could not submarines be made to zoom ahead by some form of jet propulsion? And yet the thoughtful ones were amazed by the speed and stamina of their ship.

To get the men more interested in filling out daily reports on their mental states, Dr. Weybrew showed them a chart that correlated all his findings to date. Morale fluctuated up and down. It had been high at the start of the trip, low with the illness of the Chief Radarman, high at Cape Horn, low at Friday housecleaning.

The men were not too impressed. They could have told the professor these facts without fuss or feathers. The common sense opinion of one crew member summed it all up:

"If you want morale to be high, let the men have plenty of off-duty sack time, get a place where a man can write a letter or study or play acey-deucy in peace and quiet. You won't find any boredom, then."

All kinds of comments were made to the psychologist. "How am I feeling today, Doc?" The comments were made in jest, but they disguised a real need. It was just what the investigator wanted. Many men wanted to discuss their personal problems with him, but held back because of a lack of privacy. Dr. Weybrew was convinced that submarines would do well to have a new kind of morale officer aboard—a combination of doctor and minister—to whom men under stress could turn for guidance and understanding. The list of recommendations for improvements lengthened the more the voyage was prolonged.

Heading the list was more space. A special room set aside for study, writing, and privacy was important. The sub was so crowded that "hotbunking" was necessary—two men taking turns on the same bed—one man sleeping while the other was on watch. The psychologist also felt that a small gym would be helpful. It could have weight lifting devices, rowing machines, chin bars, punching bags, and stationary bicycles equipped with timers and mileage recorders for imaginary bicycle races.

Study courses could be made more effective if text books and special credits accompanied each lecture series. Of course, there would have to be that all-important special study room. Again the submarine problem of space! But the psychologist hoped his recommendations might be used in the future expansion of the submarine program when new submarines would be built even larger than the *Triton*.

The psychologist was making a pioneer study. Snap judgments were unreliable. Years later the IBM computers would give the final answer. But it was interesting to think that kindness might some day be considered most important on a military ship. Just as metals welded together can take more stress than riveted metals (the entire *Triton* was welded), so the joining force of human kindness might withstand more stress and bring about more cooperation than any threat of punishment or any hope of reward.

The work of the hydrographers was not to solve mysteries but to collect data. The benefits that would result from an accumulation of data would come much later.

Most of the data concerned temperatures and salt content of the ocean from the surface down to different layers below the deepest point the *Triton* could submerge. In all, the hydrographers drew salinity samples from 130 points along the track of the sub. Nick Mabry proudly reported, "I covered more territory in less time than any oceanographer in history."

The data also included many uncharted mountain peaks. The hydrographers were adding to man's knowledge of the ocean bottoms. Oftentimes they wished they were able to see the majestic beauty of the unknown peaks rising from the bottom of the sea.

When the fathometer broke down, some of the hydrographers' devices proved to be valuable substitutes. One, for example, was the gravity meter, which was under the charge of geophysicist Mike Smalet. The foot-square metal box was suspended in a big wire framework to keep it steady. Mike called it his "monkey in a cage." It measured the varying pulls of gravity over the earth's surface. The deeply submerged *Triton* offered a good, steady platform unlike the to-and-fro motion of surface vessels. Whenever the submarine approached the solid mass of a submerged peak, the device recorded an increased gravity value.

The information which the *Triton* hydrographers collected was still being analyzed a year after the voyage. But so rapidly is this new science developing that within that year, the hydrographic instruments which the *Triton* carried had already come to be considered "primitive." Future submarines will have more accurate temperature gauges, more effective depth recorders, and other advanced equipment. All sorts of information will be fed into an electronic system which will add in the time, latitude, and longitude, and record everything on a paper tape.

Captain Beach was grateful for the gravity meter as well as for the sonar to warn him of the high walls of the Philippine Trench—one of the highest cliffs on the globe. The echo ranging sonar picked it up like a brick wall, and the gravity meter indicated a rapidly shoaling bottom. On March 31, the *Triton* entered Surigao Strait, the scene of one of the important naval engagements in the great Battle of Leyte.

When the hydrographers collected samples of water from the Surigao Strait, they found that it contained high concentrations of ferrous ions—in other words, rust. Captain Beach stated that the rust must have come from the Japanese battleships and cruisers sunk in the Battle of Surigao Strait. He asked the hydrographers for extra samples. One of the bottles was to go to the Naval Academy at Annapolis to join the samples of water for the annual Ring Dance, when the senior midshipmen dipped their class rings in the water of the seven seas.

Another bottle of the water was to be sent to Admiral

Jesse P. Oldendorf. It would be an emotion-packed reminder of "the finest hour" in his life. The Admiral was standing in the way of the Japanese fleet which had streamed out of Surigao Strait expecting to knock out the American occupation forces that had just landed in the Philippines. The repaired battleships of Pearl Harbor had their moment of revenge as they transformed the on-coming Japanese fleet into the rusting sunken wrecks, the evidence of which was now being collected by the hydrographers of the *Triton*.

Chapter *13*

Pilgrimage to Magellan

W hen Captain Beach had suggested in Washington that he make a side excursion to Mactan Island in the Philippines, where Magellan was killed, the admirals nodded in approval. When he reached this stage of the voyage, however, the skipper found himself with a non-functioning fathometer and without the spare parts to repair it. Navigation was going to be hazardous.

The *Triton* submerged deeply when it headed northward through Bohol Strait and the Hilutangan Channel that separated Mactan Island from the island of Cebu. During the night, the huge submarine had to use all her senses— radar, periscope, and sonar—to keep a constant check on propeller noises of passing steamers, the sides and bottom of the channel, and landmarks on the shore.

The navigators crowded the conning tower, working on star fixes to locate the sub's changing position. The navigation stars Sirius, Procyon, Aldaran, and Capella helped pinpoint the location of the ship as it snaked through the Philippines. A strong, 2-knot current forced the crew to be doubly alert.

The narrow Hilutangan Channel that separated Mactan

Island from Cebu harbor and the city of Cebu was the hardest test. It was thronged with traffic, and the *Triton* crept along at a snail's pace of four knots. Fortunately a swift current in the same direction increased the total speed to seven knots. The sonar repeater gave an exact picture of the dimensions of the channel.

During daylight hours, passengers on passing ships might have looked directly into the eye of the periscope two inches above the surface. Apparently they neither observed it nor noticed its slight wake. The waters were teeming with fishing and pleasure craft with the typical colorful odd-shaped sails of the Orient. Several great rafts of logs passed by, steered by a native at one end and driven by a hastily manufactured "sail" of branches perched at the other end.

When the *Triton* reached Magellan Bay on the north end of Mactan Island, half the circumnavigation was completed. The 71st hydrographic bottle was ejected, this time with a new wording printed on the back of the paper inside. The new inscription read, "Hail, Noble Captain. It Is Done Again." It was Captain Beach's salute to Magellan —the first circumnavigator.

A search still had to be made to find the monument that marked the tragic end of Magellan's life. Thus far every care had been taken to keep Project Magellan top secret, but this portion of the *Triton's* mission required much periscope-work in a crowded bay. The Captain suddenly found himself staring through the periscope right into the eyes of a young man in a dugout canoe.

The young fisherman, with his battered straw hat, his oar resting against the boat, was staring fixedly at the strange eye of the periscope. He was the first unauthorized person to see the top secret craft since the start of the voyage, 19,700 miles back. The skipper lowered the periscope quickly, but the photographer was at his side dying to take a picture. The periscope was raised again and the young man was still staring, looking more dazed than ever. On the third raising of the periscope, the native was paddling away with frantic haste.

Later, a member of the *National Geographic Society*, with only the periscope picture and Captain Beach's description as a guide, undertook to find and interview the fisherman. Finally, came the triumphant cable—"Have found needle in haystack." He was 19-year old Rufino Baring of Mactan Island. When the young man saw his photograph, taken through the periscope, he was shocked beyond words.

Rufino recalled that when he saw the periscope for the first time he thought it was a piece of wood. Then, seeing its wake, he was sure it was the fin of a fish. When it disappeared and rose again and he saw its malevolent shine, he was paralyzed with fear, certain that he had come across a sea monster. He was held hypnotized by the eye of the sea serpent. When it disappeared again, he raced away as if his life depended on it. He told no one of it, except a friend, who was curious to know why he had painted San Pedro and San Pablo on the side of his dugout. His explanation was that St. Peter and St. Paul were the saints who would protect him from any further encounter with sea monsters. By a curious coincidence he chose the apostles who gave their names to St. Peter and St. Paul Rocks, the islet where the circumnavigation began and where it was to be completed.

The experience with the Filipino native was a sharp reminder to Captain Beach of the immense cultural gap between the skipper of a $100,000,000 technological wonder and the simple fisherman who, through successive generations, had changed little since the days of Magellan.

When the gleaming white monument dedicated to Magellan finally burst into distant view on the south shore of Magellan Bay, the Captain stared at it with emotion. It was a rectangular pedestal with a rounded top, situated on a rise of ground, overlooking the water.

Beach felt the spiritual bond that tied the two circumnavigators through the centuries. Magellan was 41 when he died, the same as Captain Beach's age in 1960. Both had been through long years of military danger in their youths. Both were men above the common level—noble captains—who were concerned with the advancement of knowledge and the welfare of their crews. Both were men of deep spiritual faith, animated by ideals. The vast gulf of technology that separated them seemed of little importance compared to the intuitive understanding they had for each other.

Captain Beach said goodbye to the Philippines regretfully and set his course to resume the remaining half of the voyage.

Beach's father had been a lieutenant on the *Baltimore* when Admiral Dewey defeated the Spanish fleet at the Battle of Manila Bay. The elder Beach sympathized with the Filipino farmers and their leader, Aguinaldo, in their determined fight for independence. At one time he unknowingly captured Aguinaldo's young wife and a party of her servants and protectors, but in a spirit of gallantry, he allowed them to go free. Sometime later, he was captured by Filipino guerillas, and much to his surprise, he was freed and permitted to return to the American lines. Aguinaldo had returned the courtesy. Afterwards, the Filipino hero and Beach's father corresponded at intervals. For this reason alone, Captain Beach would always have a sentimental feeling for the gentle Filipinos.

In Bohol Strait, the *Triton* was back in deep water, racing toward the Pearl Bank Passage, which she reached the following noon. The passage was narrow and possibly dangerous, but fortunately a freighter going in the same direction served, unknowingly, as a guide.

The Celebes Sea and Makassar Strait brought the *Triton* into the region of the fabulous Spice Islands. A two-masted Makassar inter-island merchantman was spotted. Ships exactly like it might have been sailing the same seas in the early age of Portuguese exploration.

The passage through Lombok Strait on Tuesday, April 5, proved to be as difficult as printed navigation warnings described it to be. At several known places around the world, there is a tremendous downward flow of enormous quantities of water. The deep Mediterranean, for example, flows out over a sill near Gibraltar that separates the basin of the sea from the open Atlantic. Many subs were lost in World War II because of currents created by this dam beneath the sea.

With the *Triton* at periscope depth, the Captain was enjoying the beauties of the mountain peaks on either side of the Strait, which flows between the islands of Lombok

[167]

and Bali. Both shores could be seen clearly. A village was visible at the foot of Mt. Rindjani on Lombok, and there were verdant, cultivated terraces up the steep side of Bali. Suddenly, an oncoming ridge of water several feet high swamped the periscope. Diving Officer Jim Hay cheerfully announced he would bring the ship back up to periscope depth in a jiffy. But despite all his efforts, the depth gauges continued spinning as the submarine kept plunging down. It reached a depth of 125 feet in 40 seconds. The diving officer, who had always had fingertip control of air pressure and ballast, was flabbergasted. Only a surge of increased speed, finally, pushed the *Triton* out of the dangerous water pocket.

Like the effect of air pockets on airplanes, a powerful phenomenon of nature renders most of man's mechanisms helpless. The *Triton* had hit the point where the deep and colder waters of the Indian Ocean met the shallower, warmer waters of the Flores Sea, and tumultous vertical currents are created. The *Triton* had plunged into an undersea Niagara. With her great power there had been no real danger, but an older, less modern submarine might have had difficulty.

Triton entered the Indian Ocean on April 5 and set a great circle course for the Cape of Good Hope. At this point, she began a prolonged sealed ship experiment, including a three-day "no-smoking" ban.

Chapter *14*

The Breaking Point

The engineering spaces occupied almost two-thirds of the ship. Two propulsion systems on either side of a passageway were like massive pieces of modern sculpture. The pipes, boilers, and chrome control panels, arranged at each side of the walkway in circles, squares, and cylinders of gray, green, and cream were striking examples of a new kind of engineering.

There was none of the raucous noise, the grime and grease of the diesel-engined ships. There were no sweating, oil-smeared "snipes" (Navy slang for machinist mates) scrambling among plunging cylinders and screeching wheels. The air was clean and without odor. Only subdued sounds were heard in the brilliantly lighted rooms. A circular compartment in the center of each propulsion system housed an atomic reactor. Looking down from a metal catwalk, one could glimpse the heavily leaded, amber glass window that covered a spider web of aluminum tubing of an atomic re-actor.

The skipper could never pass by this part of the ship without a sense of awe at the mysterious power of the ghostly atomic fire. The invisible fire never seemed to consume itself. It could push his *Triton* through the seas for years without refueling. Everything was controlled by bright-colored buttons, switches, and rods that lined the control panels in abstract designs of glass and plastic.

One bank of mechanical brains stretching from floor to ceiling was called "Idiot Alley" by the crew. Only an idiot, they jokingly claimed, could understand the super-complicated gear. Captain Beach, himself, who was supposed to know something about everything in the submarine, sometimes imagined that the bewildering maze of mechanisms had a weird life of its own.

But now and then, the robot mechanisms became balky and temperamental. They required the delicate hands of a surgeon to replace a dead transistor or a punctured condenser. Sometimes a cam contact, perhaps made rusty by salt-laden sea air, required a soft massage in order to get an entire machine functioning again. The technician had to practice the tender care and intuition of a mother to keep his machine happy. Sometimes, he literally had to spank a machine. A good, hard banging might shake the parts out of a temperamental fit.

Electrician Raymond Comeau entered a revealing passage in his diary. Comeau's watch station was at the starboard turbine throttle.

"How does the turbine feel? After a while, the noise becomes a melody, different melodies. And you can tell when the turbine is happy, and when it doesn't care, and when it whines as if it were crying.

"After a while, I realize that the turbine sounds sad when I feel sad and happy when I feel happy. Does that mean that I have become, somehow, part of the machine? No! It is the slave and I am the taskmaster: I can make it purr and I can make it whine. This gives me a feeling of power . . ."

This feeling of power did not persist indefinitely. Machines were constantly rebelling. SINS was made useless by a tiny wobble of one of its gyros. The fathometer stopped functioning when a crystal cracked. A filter conked out in a radar scope. A transformer burned out. So it went every few days.

Maintenance was a never ending job on the *Triton*, with its 70 miles of cable, its 118 electric motors and its 64 miles of piping. Mechanics were constantly doctoring machines, and this fact alone persuaded Captain Beach that a machine could never take the place of a trained man.

"Automation will never replace man's brain," he wrote. "It is merely an extension of man's power. I can never have full confidence in completely automated machinery. It is bound to break down every once in a while. Trained men are better, more flexible, and more reliable. In the long run, they're cheaper, too."

No machine, however complex, should be considered more worthy of admiration than the man in charge. It was reassuring to the skipper to know that the Navy considered the morale of a crew as important as the mechanical monster that housed them.

Daily ventilation of the submarine by the snorkel device was discontinued on Sunday, April 10th, and oxygen began to be "bled" in from storage tanks. The new machines that separate oxygen from sea water were not perfected when the *Triton* was built, though later submarines were outfitted with this equipment. Revitalizing the air from oxygen tanks was expensive. There was only a limited amount of this life-sustaining gas stored away. A chemical candle composed of iron and sodium chlorate was lit in the engine room, releasing more oxygen.

Everyone felt the difference when the oxygen content was maintained at a constant level. The atmosphere was more invigorating, holding great promise for the oxygen machines of the future. The reaction to the no-smoking ban was something else again. It came on April 15th, a Friday Inspection Day, the most unpopular day of the week.

The crew started its murmuring almost immediately. The entire blame came crashing upon the psychologist, whose sole function on the ship, it was now claimed, was to invent sadistic tortures for the crew. Sixty-one percent of the crew were heavy smokers. To take the solace of tobacco from them was a personal affront. The partly humorous, partly serious resentment against being a "guinea pig" in an experiment—this experiment, at all events—mounted hour by hour. A magazine cutout was hung in a passageway, showing a blissful couple smoking. The words on the advertisement read: "Remember how cigarettes used to taste?"

Men walked about with unlit cigarettes drooping from their mouths. They drew on empty pipes. Men chewed on cigars, snuff, and great wads of chewing gum. Thirty percent of the crew reported headaches and asked for pills from the dispensary.

There was a sudden demand for a repeat of a horror

movie that had been judged the worst of the 45 films already shown. The men were more boisterous than ever in loud raspberries and mocking laughter.

The *Triton* reached the area of the Cape of Good Hope on Easter Sunday, April 17. The Plan of the Day, distributed each morning, contained a plea from the Captain for the crew to attend church services that day. But only eight officers and eight enlisted men attended Sunday services, the poorest attendance of the entire trip.

By the third day, edginess and irritability had almost reached open hostility. The crew had not been told how long the ban would last. Since there were only three square yards of deck space provided for each man, and it was difficult to move without jostling into someone else, conditions became ripe for explosion. Dr. Weybrew suggested to the Captain there was no longer any need to continue the test.

It was a delicate moment for the Captain, who had to find a way to dissipate the fractious mood of the crew with a touch of diplomacy. In this case, instead of announcing that the smoking lamp would be relit at midnight, he went about the ship smoking a cigar, and blowing the smoke in the faces of crewmen.

It took but a few seconds for the news to travel throughout the ship. There were cheers and laughter. Cigarette lighters and cigarettes popped out of pockets. It was just the right touch to dissolve all the hostility in a new aura of good humor.

Chapter *15*

Homecoming

There was no periscope liberty to see Mt. Vasco de Gama on the Cape of Good Hope. Because of currents and the need for secrecy, the *Triton* could get no nearer than eight miles from the shore. Weather conditions made photography impossible. The ship rounded the Cape and headed northwest for St. Peter and St. Paul Rocks. There the voyage would be officially completed.

The Captain had retired to his cabin to work on the log of his voyage, which he had been writing in non-technical language since the start of the trip, when someone knocked at his door, saying, "Something is wrong down in the Mess Hall Captain; we need you down there right away." The skipper jumped from his chair, almost slid down the ladder to the lower deck and rushed in to the Crew's Mess, hardly knowing what to expect. Flash bulbs blinded him and voices chanted, "Happy Birthday to You." The skipper's worried frown changed into a big smile. He joined in the spirit of the occasion by cutting the tablewide cake with a saber.

Dr. Weybrew noted a marked rise in morale during days following with the arrival of babygrams and radiograms. The happy fathers were given cigars by the skipper and babygram forms in two versions by the ship's cartoonist, Jim Smith. He drew cupids and hearts for the mother and pot-bellied old men for the father. The radiograms announced that 25 of the crew had passed their examinations for advancement in rate. Thus far during the voyage a total of 40 men had won promotions to the next higher rate—an outstanding performance for the crew the size of the *Triton's*.

The psychologist noticed the first signs of "channel fever," the unrepressed excitement that takes hold of a crew near the end of a voyage. Glorious beards began to vanish, men spoke more frequently of home, and restlessness increased. Meals once again became great events. It took three sittings to feed the whole crew, and their vocabulary described the gusto with which they attacked the pork chops and steaks. Some types of food were "oley-mooley." The 4:00 p.m. snack was "soup down." Meats were doused with "red lead" (ketchup). Coffee was "bitter and black" or "sweet and blonde."

The *Triton* had almost reached the Rocks, when near disaster struck. Allen W. Steele was standing watch in the After Torpedo Room when he heard an explosion and a heavy spraying noise. Clouds of oil vapor began to rise from beneath the deck plates. Steele grabbed the phone and reported a hydraulic oil leak in the stern plane mechanism. Then he dove down to reach for the cut-off valves of the oil supply and return pipes. The room filled with oil vapor in seconds, and visibility was reduced to a few feet. One valve shut easily, but he struggled in vain to shut the other. Just then Engineman Arlan F. Martin was at his side. Together they were able to force the valve shut. The oil flow stopped immediately.

In the control room, a crewman suddenly noticed he could not work the stern planes. The Officer of the Deck snapped out, "Shift to Emergency!" A single switch was thrown, and control of the ship was regained.

Within the same half-minute, Ronald Dale Kettlehake entered the After Torpedo Room to trace a system. Realizing the situation, he roused the dozen sleepers in the compartment, routing them forward into the engine rooms.

The Officer of the Deck had already ordered "Smoking lamp out!" and "Rig After Torpedo Room for emergency ventilation!" When the Damage Control Officer arrived in the After Torpedo Room, everything had been done according to drill instructions.

Captain Beach shivered at the thought of the narrow margin of seconds that saved the ship. A few seconds more and the heavy concentration of oil mist might have been exploded by the tiniest electric spark into a raging fire. There is nothing more horrible in a submarine than fire. There is no way to let out the toxic gases fast enough. Although each crew member had a gas mask that could be connected to compressed air outlets in each compartment, one could never be sure how long a fire would last. Men always eyed each other like hawks for any possible fire hazard.

Equally dangerous was the loss of hydraulic power. Light, fast-flowing oil confined within an enclosed space under high pressure is an easy means of moving heavy objects with finger-tip control. Such hydraulic oil pressure moves the bow and stern planes, the steering systems, all the masts and periscopes, and the vent valves of the ballast tanks. Without hydraulic oil, there is no control over the submarine. Even emergency manual control might not be effective because of the speed at which the *Triton* was moving. Within the half minute of flow out of the fractured valve, the After Torpedo Room bilges had been flooded with a foot of oil. Had Steele's action been less prompt, the *Triton* circumnavigation might have ended in disaster.

This was the second time that a valve had failed on the *Triton.* As far back as October 2, 1958, while *Triton* was still under construction, a steam valve blew out with violent force. Lieutenant Commander Kelly happened to be the engineering watch officer at that time. He, too, acted promptly. He evacuated the crew, checked the list of men, found one missing, plunged back into the steam-filled space, and led the missing man to safety.

Kelly won a Navy and Marine Corps Medal for personal heroism. The Captain, now, recommended Allen W. Steele for a letter of commendation and a commendation ribbon for meritorious service. Once again, Navy drill had paid off in saving a ship and the lives of her crew.

By noon of the following day, April 25, the *Triton* was within a few miles of St. Peter and St. Paul Rocks. By 3 p.m. the islet was circled and photographed once more. With pride, the Captain sent off a radiogram "Circumnavigation completed on schedule. Proceeding."

In his log, the skipper noted:

"Our mileage (Rock to Rock) was 26,723 nautical or 30,752 statute miles. It has taken us 60 days and 21 hours.

"Shift to Emergency!" snapped the Officer of the Deck.

Dividing gives an average speed of just over 18 knots, or 21 statute miles an hour. No other ship—and no other crew—could have done better. We are proud to have been selected to accomplish this undertaking for our nation."

The same night, officers and crew celebrated their triumph with a party featuring songs and skits. The Captain began the festivities by reading a radiogram from the Commander, Submarine Force, Atlantic Fleet:

"*Triton's* voyage around the world is indeed a tribute to the men who built such a wonderful ship but moreover it is a tribute to the submariners, the iron men who man the iron ships. History will record your submerged voyage around the world with the great exploits of the great explorers."

Amidst punch, popcorn, and pizza pies, entertainment was provided by Fireman Rudolph Kuhn, who, nearly bursting a blood vessel, played bugle calls on an instrument he created out of copper tubing and an old funnel. The skit of a TV cooking instructor, who slowly drank her "sherri-herri" sauce and fell into a televised stupor, convulsed the audience, not only because of the performance, but also because the "sherri-herri" bottle had been secretly doctored with chili sauce. The disconcerted performer did his best to conceal his anguish. What with hats and noisemakers, group singing, amateur contests, and the judging of the most glorious beard, everyone felt on top of the world even though under water.

There was no longer any pressure about maintaining strict speed and course limits, so Captain Beach was able to give the engineers an urgent drilling. A radiation leak was simulated. The ship was ventilated by the snorkel. Welders had to enclose themselves in white suits, capes over their heads, special goggles, and rubber boots. All clothing seams had to be taped together so as to leave no spot for radiation to enter. Afterwards, Dr. Stark continued the realism by having all the men monitored to determine any trace of radiation. All badges were called in to be photographed.

The *Triton* was going home by way of Cadiz, Spain, as was originally planned. The sub stopped at Tenerife, one of the Canary Islands, to practice photo reconnaissance. The lights of Santa Cruz at 4:30 a.m. had the appearance of stars because the city was so high above the water.

Photography completed, the *Triton* departed for its rendezvous with the destroyer *Weeks* just off San Lucar de Barrameda, from whence Magellan had set sail for his historic circumnavigation. The port was about 17 miles from Cadiz.

At 3:00 on the morning of May 2, the *Weeks* was sighted. The *Triton* broached her sail out of water, as she had done off Montevideo two months ago, to receive a whaleboat from the *Weeks*. The weather had begun to freshen, and the whaleboat, after several passes, rode up on a wave and crashed down on the submerged deck of the *Triton*. When the boat slid back into the sea, two men fell backward into the water. Since the ships were stopped, the men were able to climb back into the boat with ease.

After several passes, two passengers on the whaleboat managed to make flying leaps into the *Triton* deck, and a sack of mail was passed aboard. The coxswain of the boat, fearful of a serious accident in the swelling sea. decided abruptly to cast off his lines and get back to the destroyer.

[*181*]

Delivering mail by helicopter

The whaleboat had not transferred all the mail it had for the sub, and Beach radioed the destroyer skipper to get the help of helicopters standing by at Rota. Meantime Beach learned from the letters brought aboard that he was to proceed to the area of Rehobath Beach, Delaware, on May 10, which would terminate the submerged voyage.

One of the mail sacks contained the bronze plaque which had been designed by Lt. Tom Thamm of the *Triton*, and which was later to be presented to the Spanish government by John Davis Lodge, then the U.S. ambassador to Spain. The inscription on the plaque was in Latin, *Ave Nobilis Dux, Iterum Factum Est*—"Hail, Noble Captain, it is done again." The plaque was photographed and admired, then packed away again for transmission to Madrid.

[182]

The *Triton* broached again when the helicopters arrived. This time sacks of mail were easily transferred. The National Geographic photographer, Commander Roberts, together with all the film taken during the *Triton* voyage, and Commander Betzel were lifted bodily into a helicopter, which then sped away. For simplicity and security in transferring passengers and supplies, especially in heavy seas, the helicopter won hands down over the whaleboat.

The *Triton* was now on the last leg of her historic voyage —all that remained was a mere 3,000 miles across the Atlantic. This last leg turned out to be the longest of all weeks. "Channel fever" now took possession of the entire crew.

Even though the submarine had nearly completed the longest submerged trip in the history of the world, she still had enough fuel and food left to circumnavigate the world again, were it necessary, and would certainly have done it if the defense of the country had demanded it. As it was, the crew had psychologically prepared themselves for the end of the trip, and, as was their right, were eager to return to their homes.

The *Triton*, in fact, was the first ship in history to prepare for a four-month, non-stop voyage. There never was a ship, even Magellan's or the whaling ships of New England, that planned to sail more than a month without somehow receiving provisions. Although Magellan expected to take a year to reach the East Indies, he thought he could always stop at islands en route for fresh fruits and vegetables. The *Triton* had been prepared to stay under water, if need be, for as long as six months.

In this sense, Captain Beach might even be considered a forerunner of the space explorers. Once rocketed into space, moving in an alien environment, the space ship of the future would resemble the *Triton* to a remarkable degree. Nuclear reactors would power machines to produce light, water, and oxygen. Like the *Triton*, the space ship would be divided into similar compartments. One section would be crammed with basic supply stores, tanks of oxygen, water, and food. Another section would have electronic panels and automatic devices to control navigation, observation, and ship operation. There would be the same machines for removing carbon dioxide and any toxic gases.

An historian himself, Captain Beach had a sense of history. As the *Triton* moved toward the Delaware Cape, he silently saluted the brave navigators of the future who would come after him and endure the same isolation and risk along unknown paths across the silent seas of space.

He hoped—but without much certainty, however—that the navigators of the future would have a better selection of movies than had the *Triton*. Captain Beach had a good chance to appraise the movies through a second showing of the series. The most critical blows fell upon Torpedoman Second Class W. A. Jones, who ran the Wardroom movies. The Captain threatened to demote him a grade every time he showed a bad movie. Poor Jones did not have a ghost of a chance. The skipper pronounced all the movies "poor" and Jones was finally reduced to a recruit. He continued to show bad movies, and since he could not be demoted any lower, a new order of negative ranks was instituted, and Jones was progressively demoted to Negative Chief Torpedoman.

The rest of the crew, equally anguished at the movies and fully sympathizing with their skipper, demanded that when they reached port, Jones walk ashore on his hands. As a final indignity, poor Jones was told he would have to pay the Navy for the privilege of being aboard. Just before the last day, however, the skipper kindly promoted him back to his original rating, an unprecedented jump of seven grades.

On May 9, six of the crew members were awarded the coveted silver dolphins. They had learned how to operate all the systems of the *Triton* and were thus "qualified in submarines."

The last few days went by in slow motion. A chart in the Combat Center had been set up, listing the time remaining for the end of the voyage. It had begun with Minutes, 10,260; Hours, 171, Days, 7.13; Months 0.23; Years 0.0195; Centuries 0.000195. On the last two days the chart was changed hourly.

At last on Tuesday, May 10, 1960, the *Triton* surfaced. It had been submerged exactly 83 days, 10 hours, and had travelled 36,014 nautical miles. Boats and planes brought newspapermen for photographs and interviews. A helicopter deposited a sack of mail, and swept up the skipper all dressed up in a khaki uniform. He was transferred to the back lawn of the White House. While waiting for President Eisenhower, a pair of feminine arms circled his neck from the back and kissed his cheek. Whirling about, he saw the radiant face of his wife, Ingrid.

The President greeted his old friend, Ned, with a broad smile, and pinned the Legion of Merit medal on his ribbon-decked tunic. The Presidential citation stated that Captain

Eisenhower pinned the Legion of Merit on Ned Beach.

Beach had "led his crew with courage, foresight, and determination in an unprecedented circumnavigation of the globe, proving man's ability under trying conditions to accomplish prolonged, submerged missions as well as testing new and complex equipment in the world's largest submarine."

Captain Beach then flew back to the *Triton* to take her up the Thames River to a berth at the Submarine Base in New Groton, Connecticut. As the *Triton* entered the Thames River, the members of the crew, in dress uniforms, formed a solid line from bow to stern. Each man had proudly tucked away a small white card, signed by King Neptune and his servant, Edward L. Beach. The card read:

"*Know ye, all landlubbers, sea lawyers, fishmongers and other non-sea goers that blue water sailor ......, an* honorary member of the ship's company of the largest sub-marine in the world, *PRIMUS SUBCIRCUMNAVIGAVIT USS TRITON(SSR(N)586) Having on 16 February—10 May, 1960 performed feats aboard this mighty vessel, both above and below the surface of the sea, which have not heretofore been witnessed by my court and having descended into the guarded depths of my realm, shall hereafter be duly recognized for these feats and accorded the rights and privileges of a tried and true nuclear submariner.*

  Edward L. Beach   *Neptunus Rex*
   His Servant

  Flying from the highest periscope was a weatherbeaten flag. By supreme good fortune, Captain Beach had been able to borrow the ensign that flew over the *Memphis* on the dis-astrous day of her death by a tidal wave. His father's old flag proudly flapped over the ship that was returning home from the first round-the-world-under-water voyage.

  What was the most important long-range result of this amazing voyage? Captain Beach expressed it this way:

  "The important thing is to make an enemy think hard before acting. Peace may be best kept by a long, grey line of ships outside a harbor or cruising at sea—a visible dis-play of power—supplemented by a hidden weapon under a vast expanse of ocean with no ship seen from horizon to horizon. Both are important.

  "An enemy might be tempted to atom bomb our fleet in the Mediterranean, for example, or threaten to do so, so as to frighten us into a quick treaty. But now there is another string to our bow, for the invisible striking power of missiles

[*187*]

under the sea would make them pause.

"This is the significance of our having accomplished the entire voyage of the *Triton* undetected. Since the submarine—unless and until it reveals itself by attacking—is as though not there, it is a most potent weapon in the arsenal of freedom. The fact that it is invisible means that a potential enemy never knows when it might be near at hand, ready to do its job."

There was a very good reason why the *Triton* had to practice being an unseen phantom of a U. S. task force. She was specialized to go out far ahead of any fleet to seek and report contact with the enemy. Like the Indian scouts of old, the *Triton*, as a radar-picket ship, was destined for the most dangerous service of all.

She had to be faster and able to go down deeper than any submarine had gone before. She had more horse power than any World War I battleship, and more early warning devices than in an entire Navy task force of World War II days. Her radar eyes and her sonar ears could detect anything submerged, afloat, or in the air, and for greater distances than any previous subs. She was capable, under certain conditions, of giving an earlier warning of enemy attack than the DEW line of Arctic radar stations.

The tiny cabin of the Captain with its seven telephones and two public address systems might very well become, someday, the most important link in America's defense system.

The skipper, with his long record of war experience, could easily visualize what might happen on war patrols of the *Triton*. It would reconnoiter the surface off enemy shores.

There it would detect and gather information on the numbers and movements of submarines, planes, ships, and promptly radio the intelligence back to the task force behind.

An immediate submergence to incredible depths would follow. Here she could rest, secure in the knowledge that she was detection-proof under bands of water of varying temperatures. Under such layers, known as thermal layers, a submarine might move or hide unheard, unseen.

She would be able, however, to receive messages from the task force. She was equipped with special radios to receive at the very highest and lowest frequencies. If the message spelled out—"Missiles fired, what damage?" the *Triton* could surface again. Fantastic instruments would compute the damage.

This time, however, the alerted enemy might be able to detect her and take instant, computer-directed action. The engineers had planned *Triton* for just such an emergency. If the *Triton* escaped a direct hit, she would have a good chance of survival.

She was the only nuclear submarine in the Navy which was built double-hulled from bow to stern, possessing two skins of thick, hardened, welded metal. The smashing of her outer hull by pressure waves would in no way interfere with her ability to submerge and speed away.

She was divided into nine, watertight compartments and honeycombed with cubicles of all shapes and sizes. The sections were separated by hatch doors, oval in shape and as heavy as the doors of bank vaults. If an inner compartment were pierced, compressed air at tremendous pressures could hold back the flood of water. She could keep on going at

75 percent normal speed with only half her power. There were two powerful propellers to drive her.

Her twin nuclear reactors gave her double insurance. If one atomic reactor were incapacitated, there would always be the twin to provide the heat that made the steam to whirl the turbine and revolve the propellers.

No other submarine had such a specially trained repair crew, or was provided with an inventory of up to 300,000 spare parts. Such elaborate facilities for repair are usually provided only on shore. Many parts in the Triton had been built in duplicate or triplicate, so a damaged part could be automatically supplanted.

It would be possible for even a handful of survivors to use a central automatic control to bring the ship back to safety in the event of damage. The steering sticks could be locked together and one control wheel, similar to that in an airplane, could steer the Triton back home.

The Triton was born and was built for some possible moment of supreme urgency in the future. If that moment should ever come, her Captain must be the indispensible heart, soul, and brain of the Triton. His would be the awesome responsibility in a moment of crisis. His split second decision could mean life or death for the crew and the ship. It might even mean victory or defeat for the free world.

At all times, U.S. submarines—the Triton and her sister ships—are cruising in the free oceans of the free world. It is their natural heritage which all of the ships of the United States Navy will ever defend.